Open Letters

to Catholic Graduates

Open Letters to Catholic Graduates

PAUL LAVIN, PH.D.

RAFKA PRESS
PHOENIX, AZ

Copyright © 2017 Paul Lavin, Ph.D.

Typesetting, layout, cover design, copyright © 2017 Rafka Press LLC

All rights reserved. No part of this book may be reproduced or transmitted in any form or by any means, electronic or mechanical, including photocopying, recording, or by any information storage or retrieval system now existing or to be invented, without written permission from the respective copyright holder(s), except for the inclusion of brief quotations in a review.

The Scripture citations used in this work are taken from the *Saint Joseph New Catholic Edition of the HOLY BIBLE,* Copyright © 1962 by Catholic Book Publishing Company, NY.

Published by
Rafka Press LLC
Phoenix, Arizona, USA

ISBN-13: 978-0-9911958-8-6

Library of Congress Control Number: 2017943513

10 9 8 7 6 5 4 3 2 1

Visit us online at www.rafkapress.com
For more information: info@rafkapress.com

Dedication

Open Letters to Catholic Graduates is dedicated to John Vennari, editor of Catholic Family News (CFN). It was John Vennari who inspired me to write this book. This journey began in April 2015. Mr. Vennari published my article, "An Open Letter to the Graduating Class of 2015," which focused on the challenges young Catholics would face when entering the secular world. In my communication with Mr. Vennari, he referred to the Open Letter as "first rate" and "really terrific." Needless to say, Mr. Vennari's comments were not only uplifting but inspirational. Following this, another Open Letter addressed to Catholic graduates entering college was then published in the May 2015 edition of CFN, and so the project began and ended two years later.

Thank you, John Vennari. You were the catalyst, leading to the completion of this book. Without your support and encouragement, *Open Letters to Catholic Graduates* would never have become a reality. God bless you and CFN!

I was deeply saddened when I heard that Mr. Vennari passed away just before *Open Letters to Catholic Graduates* went to press. He never saw the completed book. John Vennari will be sorely missed by those of us who worked with him. May his soul RIP.

Contents

1 ... Introduction

I
Open letters to Catholic graduates preparing to enter secular society

7 ... To those young Catholic men and women who will soon be entering secular society

15 ... On the importance of reaffirming life's purpose

21 ... To those graduates attending a secular college or university

29 ... On the importance of taking the devil and hell seriously

35 ... On the importance of prayer and persistence

43 ... On forming true friendships in a secular world

49 ... On caution: beware of those who are Catholic in name only

II
Open letters on the capital sins and temptation

55 ... On the capital sins and how the devil uses them

61 ... On pride, the father from which all sins arise

71 ... On the capital sin of greed and
the importance of charity

79 ... On the capital sin of anger and how
this can lead to hate and revenge

85 ... On the capital sin of gluttony —
"getting wasted"

93 ... On the capital sin of sloth and the danger
of becoming spiritually slothful

99 ... On the capital sin of lust — the
devil's favorite weapon

III
Open letter on how psychology can help you

129 ... On using Catholic psychology
to combat capital sins

IV
Open letter on preparing for the end of life

149 ... On the final judgment

Introduction

This book of Open Letters was written for you, those young Catholic men and women who are preparing to enter secular society. While this journey will be exciting, you will be facing a lot of challenges along the way. This book will focus on these challenges.

The first and foremost challenge will be continuing to practice your Catholic Faith in a world which is becoming more hostile toward Jesus Christ and His Church. Right now you are standing at a spiritual crossroad. The first road, which is the more attractive of the two, could easily lead you astray. The devil, who is the architect of this road, has made sure that the first road is well-paved, wide, and filled with worldly pleasures, glittering adventures, and exciting distractions. These could quickly absorb all of your time and attention.

The other road, which is far less traveled, is unpaved, rocky, and filled with potholes. If you are not careful, the potholes could trip you up, making your journey a slow and difficult one. You know that circumventing each pothole will be a challenge that is not easy to overcome. However, with each success, you know that your faith in God will be strengthened. By cooperating with God's grace, you know that you will become more adept in overcoming each challenge as it arises. The devil, on the other hand, hopes that when you see the potholes you will become discouraged. He wants you to take the easier road. You know that if you stay on the less-traveled road, your strength will continue to increase and you can complete your journey successfully. But the well-traveled road looks so attractive and easy. Suppose you were asked to choose one of the two roads. Which road would you choose? Why?

If you have decided to read this book, chances are that you would select the road less-traveled. Over the past two decades, you have been brought up in the Catholic Faith. You have received the sacraments, learned to pray, and followed the teachings of the one, holy, catholic, and apostolic Church founded by Our Lord, Jesus Christ. When you received the sacrament of Confirmation, you became a "Soldier for Christ" — a disciple of Our Lord we might say. Being chosen as a disciple is an honor — an honor of which you should be proud. It is you, the next generation of young, vibrant Catholics, who will exemplify the best of what our Faith has to offer in a world steeped in the sins of Pride and Presumption.

As you read this book of Open Letters, you will notice that I refer to each of you as "the salt of the earth" and "the light of the world." Our Lord's words in the Gospel of Saint Matthew (5:13-16) were meant for you, even though they were spoken two thousand years ago. Consider the following, which applies to you and your mission here on earth:

> [At that time, Jesus said to His disciples,] "You are the salt of the earth; but what if the salt loses its strength, what shall it be salted with? It is no longer of any use but to be thrown out and trodden underfoot by men. You are the light of the world. A city on a mountain cannot be hidden. Neither do men light a lamp and put it under a measure, but upon the lamp-stand, so to give light in to all in the house. Even so let your light shine before men, in order that they may see your good works and give glory to your Father in heaven..."

Keep this Gospel in mind as you prepare to enter secular society. Make sure that you continue to receive the sacraments so that you, "the salt of the earth" and "the light of the world," maintain your strength. The world needs your youthful zeal more than ever.

God bless you, disciples of Our Lord, "the salt of the earth" and "the light of the world." Let your light shine by your example.

I

Open letters to Catholic graduates preparing to enter secular society

To those young Catholic men and women who will soon be entering secular society

FROM: PAUL LAVIN, PH.D.

Dear Graduate,

This letter is addressed to you—the young Catholic student who will soon be leaving home and entering the world. Perhaps you will be attending a college or university, learning a trade, or working at a job in the public or private sector. While this can be a new and exciting venture, it is a journey for which you will need to be prepared. The purpose of this letter is to stimulate your thinking about those challenges you will be facing and how you, a practicing Catholic, can maintain your Faith in the years to come.

Let me begin on a sad note, of which many of you are aware. Many young Catholic men and women, like you, become far less fervent in practicing their Faith once they leave home. They may stop attending Mass, fail to receive the sacraments, discontinue praying, and give up the Faith altogether. This is not an uncommon occurrence in today's society. The temptations to leave the Church are great, and the unprepared person can easily fall prey to them.

Even though some young people succumb to earthly temptations and leave the Church, this does not mean that the world is a gloomy place, from which you must hide or be constantly fearful. On the contrary! God created the world and everything in it. Therefore, it is filled with much good, provided that we use God's creation as He intended.

As I stated earlier, the purpose of this letter is to help you to face and overcome the many challenges that you can expect to encounter upon entering the world, which is often referred to as "secular society." The secular society which you will be entering is concerned with our present life here on earth and the pursuit of worldly happiness. Secular society is not concerned with religion, the salvation of your soul, or that which is sacred to God. Enjoying worldly pleasures, acquiring wealth, attaining professional and social status, and achieving happiness here on earth are the goals for which secular-thinking people strive. Secular-thinking persons may be kind and considerate. They may perform many acts of charity and help the less fortunate. However, while these deeds are praiseworthy, they are done due to an attachment to mankind, not for the love of God.

Right now you are probably surrounded by parents, relatives, and friends who, like you, are practicing Catholics. Catholic teaching encompasses almost all facets of your life. Saying Grace before and after meals, morning and evening prayers, going to Mass and receiving Holy

Communion, the recitation of the rosary, frequent Confession, and devotion to Our Blessed Mother and the saints are a normal part of your everyday life.

Your Catholic upbringing has taught you to not only be aware of God's commandments, but also the importance of being diligent in keeping them. You have been taught that God is merciful and that He loves each and every one of us. However, besides being merciful, God is just, as well. Like our loving father here on earth, God expects us to obey His laws throughout our lifetime. Those who persist in this difficult task will be rewarded by going to Heaven. Those who fail to obey God will end up in Hell. This is what Our Lord has said time and time again. The good thing is that God promised not to abandon us. He promised to give each of us the sufficient grace needed to save our souls. Notice that God doesn't force us to accept His grace or follow His laws. He has given us a free will to accept Him and His Church. He will not make us do that which we do not want to do. We can cooperate with God's plan or reject it—the choice is ours.

Keep in mind that much of the preceding will change once you enter the secular world. You will be entering a society in which people have been taught that worldly happiness comes first. You will be told that God and His laws should not interfere with this goal. Because God loves us and is merciful, you will be told that He would never condemn anyone to a place like Hell. You will be encouraged to relax your moral standards and not take life so seriously. You will be bombarded with phrases such as, "lighten up" and "go with the flow." You will be told to "chill out and not be so up-tight," and to "loosen up and have some fun." And when you see others behaving immorally, you will be told that "it's no big deal" and "everybody does it." These are just a few of the excuses or rationalizations that people will use to justify their sinful actions.

It is difficult to resist this kind of thinking because the people who encourage you to think in this way will appear to be friendly and sincere. They will seem to be happy, popular, self-confident, and content with the direction that their lives have taken. They will hardly look like the devil that we see depicted with horns and expanded nostrils breathing fire. Like you, these young people will be energetic and intelligent. This is what will make saying NO! so difficult. It is normal to want to be "cool" and to fit in. So you may be tempted to "go along to get along." This can easily become the motivation for lowering your moral standards, behaving sinfully, and corrupting your soul.

The worst part of becoming corrupted is that you won't even recognize that this is happening to you. Like a thief in the night, corruption sneaks up on you. It takes away your innocence before you realize what is happening. One sinful transgression easily leads to another and then another. Repeatedly-sinful behavior clouds your mind and warps your judgment. It dulls your conscience and you lose your sense of right and wrong. But worst of all, it impairs your relationship with God and leads you away from Him.

Let me return to my mentioning of the devil. Unlike it was in the past, the existence of the devil is currently not taken seriously and his influence on human events is either minimized or ignored. This is a major mistake! Today, more than ever, Satan is left undeterred in his efforts to spread evil throughout the world. Keep in mind that the devil's goal is to capture your soul. In order to succeed in this endeavor, he will make worldly goods appear to be much more attractive than the true practice of your Catholic Faith. The more importance that you attach to achieving worldly goals, the less likely you will be to invest time and energy in praying and receiving the sacraments. Remember that Satan is called the Father of Lies for good reason. He is extremely clever in making evil appear as good and vice versa. Don't let him trick you into submission.

In summation, as a practicing Catholic you know that the purpose of life is the salvation of your soul. Your view will not be the same as those persons who do not share your Catholic Faith. They will not agree that the salvation of one's soul is the most important priority in life. Moreover, many will argue that there is no God or life after death. If there is a God, they will contend that He is so merciful that He would never send anyone to Hell. These unfortunate persons suffer from the sin of presumption. Because they perform good deeds, they insist that God will not condemn them, even if they have violated His laws and those of His Church. As a result of such thinking, many people no longer fear God or His justice. If they have no fear of God, they will have no fear of the devil either. Denying or minimizing the influence of the devil and the reality of Hell are most dangerous to the salvation of one's soul. The devil, who is the Master of Deceit, is extremely effective in capturing the souls of those who fail to recognize his great powers of intellect and his ability to deceive human beings and lure them into damnation.

In conclusion, let me again emphasize that once you graduate, you will be entering a world which is quite different than what you have previously experienced. For the most part, you are now surrounded by an all-encompassing Catholic environment, which is designed to ward off the devil and his minions. Take a few minutes and reflect on all that God has given you to nourish and protect your Faith: parents who care about your spiritual welfare; frequent Mass and Holy Communion; frequent confession; daily prayers including the rosary; devotion to Our Blessed Mother and the saints. I'm sure that many of you could add to this list. It is your daily practicing of your Catholic Faith that has kept the devil at bay throughout your most formidable years. Right now, he is patiently waiting until the circumstances are better suited to luring you away with his false promises. Your entrance into the secular world and the pomp, dazzling glitz, and enticing pleasures that it offers might turn the odds in his favor—at least that's what the Father of Lies hopes.

Lastly, the time to think about the future is now. If you are not mentally and spiritually prepared to sustain and defend your Faith, you can easily be caught off guard by those who are hostile toward the Catholic Church or any religion for that matter. Being caught off guard can make you appear to be foolish. This, in turn, can lead to feelings of inferiority, especially if your adversaries poke fun at you and openly ridicule your beliefs. Confused thinking, shameful feelings associated with being a Catholic, and an eventual disregarding or losing of the Faith can soon follow. The Father of Lies will, of course, rejoice at achieving this goal.

As you can see, a well thought-out plan should be devised before, not after, you have entered the secular world. Remember when you received the sacrament of Confirmation. On that day you became a "Soldier for Christ." This not only intensified your bonding with God and His Church, but it further assured that your relationship with the Holy Ghost would be strengthened and that He would confer special gifts upon you. Those gifts, as you recall, are wisdom, understanding, counsel, knowledge, fortitude, piety, and fear of the Lord. Now is the time to call upon the Holy Spirit to help you to use these gifts so that you will have the strength to defend your Catholic Faith and to remain true to those vows that you have taken. May God bless you in this endeavor.

Congratulations to you, a Catholic graduate. As Our Lord said in the Sermon on the Mount: "You are the salt of the earth" and "the light of the world," upon which the Catholic Faith, by your example, will flourish.

On the importance of reaffirming life's purpose

FROM: PAUL LAVIN, PH.D.

Dear Graduate,

n my first Open Letter, I emphasized that once you enter the secular world, your life could quickly and easily change. Remember, secular-thinking persons have been taught that attaining worldly happiness is the number one priority in life and that God and His Church should not interfere with the pursuit of this goal. You, on the other hand, have been taught that God and His Church come first. The salvation of your soul, which lives for eternity, should be the first and foremost priority. Saving your soul, not the quest for "pleasure, power, and possessions," the triple concupiscence, is the purpose of life.

Keep in mind that the large majority of human beings live for the present moment. Life's purpose, from their point of view, will be engaging in activities such as the following: the pursuit of money; sensual pleasure; enjoying friends; traveling throughout the world; fame; earning academic degrees and becoming an expert in their field; finding satisfying employment; performing charitable services for the less fortunate, etc. I'm sure that you could identify a number of other worldly pursuits that could lead you to achieving happiness here on earth. As I indicated in my previous Open Letter, the preceding activities are not necessarily evil. Rather, they can be beneficial to you and do much good for others provided that you acquire and use them as God intended. If you become self-indulgent and violate God's laws in pursuing these earthly goods, however, you could damn your soul for eternity.

You should ask, "What is the purpose of life?" This is the most important question you will ever answer. Your answer to this question will determine how you live and the path that you will follow in the pursuit of true happiness, a goal for which all human beings strive. Reaffirming life's purpose means repeatedly reminding yourself why God has placed you on this earth and what He has planned for you — eternal happiness with Him in Heaven. Moreover, reaffirming life's purpose will help you to stay on track and avoid those sinful attractions that could put the salvation of your soul in great danger. Remember to keep your eyes affixed on the prize that God has promised you. Don't let Satan and his minions pull you into the pits of fire on the left and right sides of the path leading you to paradise.

Once again, let me stress that your view on the purpose of life will not be the same as those persons who do not share your Catholic Faith. Keep in mind that many of the people who live, study, and work in the world have differing beliefs on how life should be lived. As noted previously, they will not agree that the purpose of life is to save their soul. Moreover, some will argue that there is no God or any life after death. Reaffirming life's purpose will help you to stand strong when your adversaries assault Jesus Christ and the Catholic Church, which He founded.

Finally, in your repeated reaffirmation of life's purpose, focusing on Christ's words and keeping what He said at the forefront of your thoughts can help to strengthen your resolve. Let's see what Our Lord had to say about life's purpose. If there is any doubt that the purpose of life is to save your soul, consider the following, which is taken from the Gospel of Saint Matthew (16:24-27).

> [At that time, Jesus said to His disciples,] "If anyone wishes to come after me, let him deny himself, and take up his cross and follow me. For he would have his life will lose it, but he who loses his life for my sake will find it. For what does it profit a man if he gain the whole world, but suffer the loss of his soul? Or what will a man give in exchange for his soul? For the Son of Man is to come with his angels in the glory of his Father, and then will he render to everyone according to his conduct."

Christ, in this Gospel passage, speaks clearly and forthrightly about the purpose of life. He also tells us what we must do to achieve this goal. Notice that Christ proclaims that we must deny ourselves and take up our cross and follow Him.

He did not say that self-indulgence, the failure to follow His example, and ignoring His laws would lead us into Heaven. Rather, He stated, "he who loses his life for my sake will find it." In other words, Christ expects to be the number one priority in our lives; second, third, or fourth position will not do. In order to emphasize this even more forthrightly, consider the following from Saint Matthew, Chapter 10:34-42.

> [At that time, Jesus said to His disciples,] "Do not think that I have come to bring peace upon the earth. I have come to bring a sword, not peace. For I have come to set a man at variance with his father, and a daughter with her mother, and a daughter-in-law with her mother-in-law, and a man's enemies will be of his own household. He who loves father and mother more than me is not worthy of me. He who loves son or daughter more than me is not worthy of me. And he who does not take up his cross and follow me is not worthy of me. He who finds his life will lose it, and he who loses his life for my sake will find it."

This Gospel passage emphatically proclaims that Christ expects us to make Him the most important priority in our life here on earth. When we are in a Catholic community, in which everyone thinks the same way, this is relatively easy. However, imagine proclaiming these Gospel messages to the secular world, which you will soon be entering. How do you think that the majority of people would react to Our Lord's words? How might they react to you if they know that you believe what Christ stated? Reflect on this. How you react could have a major impact on your ability to stand strong in the face of secular scorn and criticism.

Lastly, Our Lord warned us that the greedy pursuit of material goods will be of no value in saving our soul. In fact, our dogged persistence and dedication to acquiring these can easily lead to making them the number one priority in our lives. Consider the following taken from Saint Luke, Chapter 12:32-34.

> [At that time, Jesus said to His disciples,] "Do not be afraid little flock. For it has pleased your Father to give you the kingdom. Sell what you have and give alms. Make for yourselves purses that do not grow old, a treasure unfailing in Heaven, where neither thief draws near nor moth destroys. For where your treasure is, there also will your heart be."

Again, Our Lord clearly states that the saving of our soul must be our first and foremost priority. Reflect on this. Where do you think most people's hearts happen to be? Where is their treasure? Keep in mind that what people treasure has a powerful influence on how they think and act. This will also have a powerful influence on how you respond when you are in their company. Make sure that the continuing reaffirmation of life's purpose is the top priority in your life.

Remember you are "the salt of the earth" and "the light of the world." Carry out Our Lord's message by your example.

To those graduates attending a secular college or university

FROM: PAUL LAVIN, PH.D.

Dear Graduate,

Many of you will be planning to attend a secular institution of higher learning upon graduation. Continuing to practice your Catholic Faith will be a challenge when this time comes. The secular college or university that you attend will be filled with well-educated, energetic, and intelligent students. They, like you, will be idealistic and want to make a positive impact on the world. Your desire to make the world a better and happier place is natural and will be shared by most of the young people with whom you come in contact. However, even though you share this common bond, there is a danger of which you should be aware. When you enter the secular world, it is easy to gradually blend into the surrounding environment, "going along to get along," you might say. If you are not careful, you could unconsciously wind up putting your Faith on the back burner — the back burner being a place where others cannot or are not likely to see it. In fact, you might appear to be so secular to your new friends that they would be surprised to find out you are a practicing Catholic who takes the Faith seriously.

Remember, Our Lord expects you to be "the light of the world." He wants you to shine so that others can profit from your example. Our Lord surely does not want you to "walk in the darkness" or hide your light so that others cannot see it. In order to keep this from happening, it is important to keep in mind that Our Lord wants you to be happy, not only with Him in Heaven, but on this earth as well. This is why He died for our sins and founded the Catholic Church—a perfect Church, which, if we follow Its teachings, will lead all of mankind to happiness both in the "here and now" and for eternity. It is important to keep this thought in the forefront of your mind so that you don't gradually slip into the "going along to get along" mentality, which is so prevalent today.

As I stated in the previous Open Letter, the large majority of secular students, with whom you associate, will have markedly different views on what constitutes happiness and how to go about achieving it. Remember the triple concupiscence "pleasure, power, possessions"? Secular-thinking people believe that these constitute happiness. Moreover, many believe that "the end justifies the means" — that it is acceptable to violate God's laws and those of His Church to obtain those things which they think will make them happy.

As I indicated to you in my first Open Letter, because you are a Confirmed Catholic—a Soldier for Christ—you will be different than most young people who attend a secular school. The chances are good that you will be confronted by many persons who do not believe that the Catholic Church is the one true Church founded by Jesus Christ. They will fail to recognize that Jesus Christ, the Son of God, and the Church that He created right here on earth, are perfect and without a blemish. They will not understand that the Catholic Church possesses all of those sacraments needed for the salvation of souls and will lead them to the happiness which they seek. Lastly, they will not understand that Christ's Church is perfect because Our Lord, Who is perfect Himself, could not create anything that was flawed. To do so would be contrary to His nature.

Because God created a perfect Church, He expects all of mankind to become members of It. This is why He sent His Apostles throughout the world. He wants all men to become baptized, receive the sacraments, and worship Him in the Church He created. Our Lord preached that the Catholic Church, and only the Catholic Church, was the road leading to the salvation of one's soul.

It is important to keep in mind that although God and His Church are perfect, this does not mean the members of It are perfect as well. God's Church can become corrupted by the sinful behavior of Its members and clergy. However, any corruption that takes place in the Church comes from man, not God. Hence, it is the people within the Church who are corrupt. The Church Itself, because it was created by Our Lord, remains perfect, regardless of Its members' sinful behavior.

In order to understand this more fully, you might compare the Church to a perfectly-designed automobile. The car runs smoothly and has no mechanical defects. But let us suppose that the owner drives the car carelessly and fails to properly maintain it. The car might still be able to transport the owner from one place to another. Instead of operating efficiently, however, it now sputters, lurches, and runs poorly. Because of the owner's negligence, the car cannot function up to its potential. Eventually, if it continues to be poorly maintained, it shall breakdown and need expensive repairs in order to restore its proper functioning. As this example shows, there were no flaws in the automobile itself causing it to become dysfunctional. Rather, it was the owner's carelessness that caused the problem.

The Catholic Church might be compared to the preceding. Christ's Church has the potential to function perfectly provided that Its members and the clergy follow God's laws. When they behave sinfully, however, the Church's veracity becomes compromised and Its ability to fulfill Its mission is undermined. For instance, the recent scandals involving the sordid behavior of some of the clergy have severely tarnished the reputation of the priesthood. Their sinful actions have undermined trust in the Church's ability to serve as a moral example to others. Moreover, it has cost millions of dollars to pay for the harm caused to innocent victims. Despite this, however, the point to keep in mind is that even though these priests behaved sinfully, this does not detract from the Church as being a perfect society. Rather, it simply points out that the scandalous behavior of men detracts from Its ability to function perfectly as Our Lord intended.

Unfortunately, throughout the many centuries of the Church's history, there have been popes, cardinals, bishops, and priests who have set bad examples and behaved sinfully. While they are in the minority, their scandalous behavior is quickly noticed and publicized by various news outlets. Their sinful actions are then paraded before the general public. The hypocrisy of the clergy not only brings disgrace on them, but it undermines the Church's credibility as well.

The laity, who see the sinful actions of their clergy, can easily lose confidence in the priesthood itself. Not only is the clergy's sinful behavior an embarrassment to them, but it reflects negatively on the Catholic Church, to which they are committed. Non-Catholics and the enemies of the Church, on the other hand, will respond gleefully when this occurs. This enables them to feel fully justified in criticizing the clergy and their superiors. Moreover, the dogma that "outside the Catholic Church there is no salvation" can be attacked as well. Scandal only affirms what they want to believe: that one religion (or no religion at all) is just as good as another.

As indicated previously, those of you who attend a secular school of higher learning are likely to hear criticisms about the Church and the clergy and hierarchy who govern It. Your peers, professors, and other members of the academic community will be up-to-date on the scandalous behavior of those priests who sodomized children, stole money from the parish funds, lived luxuriously, and abused their positions of authority. Unfortunately, the charges that they levy will be true, and you will not be able to justify such sinful actions. This will be a time in which you will be severely tested. You will be required to suffer in silence without losing your Faith in the process. Pray for the strength to endure this temptation, and for those who are the enemies of Our Lord's Church.

To compound the problem, the intellectuals who confront you will cite secular sources to try and refute the Church's teachings. They will claim that the Church is dogmatic, authoritarian, and archaic in its views. The Catholic Church is "behind the times," they will insist. Their arguments will be articulately presented and clothed in a garment of authenticity which is called "scholarship." The Church's actions during the Crusades, the Inquisition, and the Holocaust will be attacked. Evolution, same-sex marriage, birth control, and abortion will be promoted. Again, secular sources will be cited to affirm that the Church is not only in error, but is pursuing a selfish agenda at the expense of innocent people who are being victimized by it.

If you are not prepared, you can easily be seduced by what is presented. The Church, Its teachings, the clergy, and those who are dedicated Catholics will look foolish in your eyes. You will feel shame for being a Catholic, and you will view yourself as being a stupid, uninformed dolt in comparison to those so-called "intellectuals" who appear so much smarter than you. The temptation to give up the Faith will be great. You too will want to join the "intellectual elite" who place themselves above God and His Church. Remember Eve and how she was influenced by the devil? "Pride goeth before the fall" (Proverbs 16:18). Don't let false pride lure you away from your Catholic Faith.

In order to combat the preceding: remember that when you received the sacrament of Confirmation, you became a "Soldier for Christ," and you will need to arm yourself accordingly. This will require that you read the works of Catholic historians, philosophers, and theologians. Perhaps you could talk with a priest, teacher, or trusted adult who could mentor you in this regard. Keep in mind that secular individuals will be well-prepared to educate you on the "dark side" of the Catholic Church, claiming that It has stifled human progress. You, on the other hand, need to know the Catholic point of view and the great contributions that the Church has made in the civilizations of society over the past two thousand years. As a well-educated Catholic, you will have more than ample intellectual ammunition to shoot holes in their specious and jaded arguments.

Be prepared to be fed a diet of half-truths, distortions, and lies in an attempt to lead you away from your Faith. Don't let this happen. Make sure that you read the Catholic side of the story before leaping into believing the secular world's view of current events and the history surrounding them. Knowing your Catholic heritage and the saintly men and women who are part of it will serve you well when challenges to your Faith arise!

May Saint Michael, the Archangel, protect you, "the salt of the earth" and "the light of the world," in defending Our Lord and His Church from His secular enemies.

On the importance of taking the devil and hell seriously

FROM: PAUL LAVIN, PH.D.

Dear Graduate,

n my first Open Letter, I commented on the devil and how he goes about the earth seeking the ruin of souls. Because Satan has such a powerful influence in the secular world, I would like to share some thoughts with you on this important matter. As I indicated previously, people took the devil more seriously in years gone by. They not only believed in his existence, but were taught that he actually roamed the earth, corrupting men's souls and leading them into Hell. The devil and Hell were considered to be real, not the figment of man's imagination. The thought of being corrupted by Satan and cast for eternity into an unceasing, unquenchable fire was so frightening that many people thought twice before engaging in sinful behavior.

Today the existence of the devil and the notion that corrupted souls will be condemned to Hell are ignored or taken lightly. The fear of Satan and being punished for violating God's laws has considerably lessened. As a result, sinful temptation is now brazenly paraded before us in movies, television programs, on the Internet, and in various forms of printed media. Foul language, sexual promiscuity, self-indulgence, and violence are so commonplace we fail to recognize how corrupt we have become. Shame and guilt, the unpleasant reminders following our wrong-doing, have become so dulled that they no longer serve as a deterrent to sinful behavior. Stay alert! Don't let yourself become an unsuspecting victim who naively falls into the custom-made trap which Satan has prepared for you.

You will recall that in the previous Open Letters, I said that if you lived in a Catholic community and frequently received the sacraments, it was harder for the devil to lure you into committing mortal sins and giving up the practice of your Faith. As noted earlier, however, the devil is a fallen angel with great powers of the intellect. He has an in-depth understanding of human nature and knows how to manipulate us so that we will behave sinfully.

The devil is a "Master of Deceit." He is an expert at making lies appear as truth and truth appear as lies. Moreover, the devil is highly skilled in making evil acts and material goods appear to be very attractive. This attraction can be so strong and compelling that you may be hardly able to resist it. Without prayer and the sacraments, your resistance can begin to weaken and you are likely to give in to your sinful impulses. Again, if you fail to think about this and prepare accordingly, you can easily fall victim to Satan's allure. In fact, if you are unprepared, you might not even recognize that he is manipulating you and setting a trap for your damnation.

Keep in mind that the attraction of the so-called "good" that Satan offers always appears to be much better than it is. Sin, although it might provide temporary pleasure, usually leaves us with a feeling of emptiness and disappointment after we have given in to the temptation. After the evil act is done, it is not unusual for a person to say to himself, "Is that all that this has to offer?" The results of our sinful behavior often fail to live up to our expectations.

In fact, in all likelihood you will feel cheated and angry with yourself for falling into the devil's trap. If you doubt this, think about our first parents, Adam and Eve. In order to understand how the devil works, refer to the Book of Genesis, Chapter 3:1. As you may recall, the devil took the form of a serpent. He is described as more "cunning than any beast of the field which the Lord had made." In other words, the serpent was a clever, conniving creature plotting on how he could out-smart the unsuspecting and innocent Eve. The serpent knew that he had to trick Eve in order to get her to disobey God. So what did the serpent do? He acted like an innocent creature by attempting to engage Eve in a friendly conversation with him.

The serpent began their discourse by asking what appeared to be a harmless question: "Did God say, you shall not eat of the tree in the garden?" The serpent knew the answer to the question, but he used this as a lure to entice Eve to converse with him. Eve, who was naïve and trusting, thought that the serpent was sincere in his inquiry. She then answered the question, hardly suspecting that he would use the answer to deceive her. That is what the serpent did. The serpent twisted the words so that they appealed to Eve's pride. He promised her that if she ate the fruit from the one tree that God denied them that they, too, would be like God.

By listening to the serpent and allowing herself to be tempted by him, Eve placed herself in mortal danger. The more that she thought about the serpent's promise, the more attractive this one tree became. The serpent made this one particular tree appear "more pleasing to the eye and desirable" than all the other trees. Note verse 6 from Chapter 3 in the Book of Genesis: "Now the woman saw that the tree was good for food, pleasing to the eyes, and desirable for the knowledge that it would give." You know the rest of the story. Eve disobeyed God and lured Adam into doing the same. The serpent's promises never lived up to their expectations. Rather, Adam and Eve were banned from the Garden of Eden, and they and their offspring were to suffer until the end of time. The serpent achieved this objective by lying and making sin appear to be more attractive than it really is. This is why the devil, who took on the form of a serpent, is called the Father of Lies.

It is important to note that even though the serpent tricked Adam and Eve, God held them accountable for their behavior. Eve blamed the serpent for deceiving her, and Adam blamed Eve for enticing him to eat the forbidden fruit. What Adam and Eve said was true. However, God did not accept these excuses for disobeying Him. He punished them for their sinful behavior. Could we expect that God would treat us any differently? How would God respond to the excuse "everybody does it" or "you have to go along to get along," which we hear so frequently today? Would He accept this or punish us for our sinful actions? It is best to think about this now before the Father of Lies tries to deceive you with false promises.

Some questions that you might ask yourself are as follows: If God gave Adam and Eve a second chance, would they have eaten the forbidden fruit? Did the result of their disobedience to God produce the "good" that they expected? Were they happy with their choice or did they feel cheated and remorseful following their sinful behavior? How did the devil catch them off guard and manipulate them? Examine the devil's words and actions. Could the devil use these manipulative tactics with you, especially if he knew your weaknesses and how to exploit them? Be alert to what goes on around you. Don't become so steeped in pride that you underestimate the power of Satan. The failure to be spiritually diligent, or believing that you are smarter the devil, could get you into serious trouble. And this could come about without you realizing that it is happening to you.

A simple example of how things can look much better than they really are occurs when you go to a bakery. How often have you seen a delicious-looking pastry, which can be most tempting. If you are a person on a diet, who is trying to control your weight, the temptation to indulge yourself could be great. How often do we give in and eat the pastry, only to discover that it didn't taste nearly as good as it looked? And what follows this behavior? Often we feel disappointed and wish that we had resisted the urge to indulge ourselves. The aftermath of guilt is all that remains, and the tastiness of the pastry fades further and further into the background. This is how sin works, and the devil is its master.

In conclusion, make sure that you take the devil and his great power seriously. Continue to reaffirm your Faith and keep your eyes affixed on the prize, which is the promise that God has made to you, his loyal servant. Frequent reception of the sacraments coupled with prayer, especially the rosary, are the spiritual weaponry which will help you to defeat Satan and save your soul.

May Saint Joseph, the Terror of Demons, protect you, the "salt of the earth" and "the light of the world" upon your entry into secular society.

On the importance of prayer and persistence

FROM: PAUL LAVIN, PH.D.

Dear Graduate,

Today's Open Letter will focus on prayer — a topic which was previously touched upon. The importance of prayer is given little consideration in secular society. Although "God Bless America" is sung at some sporting events, God and prayer are largely ignored by the general public. Your situation, as noted in previous Open Letters, is very different in this regard. Because you are in an all-encompassing Catholic environment, saying prayers has become a well-ingrained habit. Morning and evening prayers, Grace before and after meals, and the rosary are said daily. *Not* saying your prayers would hardly, if ever, be given a second thought. Your parents, teachers, and classmates all participate in prayer, which is expected.

Beside your daily prayers, you probably pray to God asking Him to grant wishes which you think will make you happy. Perhaps you ask Our Lord to help you to get better grades at school. Or maybe you ask to be more talented in athletics, music, or art. If you are like I was as a child, you probably tried to bargain with Our Lord for special favors: "Oh God! If you will grant me this one wish, I will go to Mass every day next week." You will notice that I tried to trade with Our Lord. My main focus was on getting what I wanted, not on what God willed for me. I suspect that Our Lord, like my father here on earth, granted many of my wishes, which just happened to make me momentarily happy. The fulfillment of my wishes probably coincided with God's plan on how He wanted me to live my life at that time. Otherwise, my requests would not have been granted, at least not in the way that I thought they should be. In my youthful years, this slipped right by me. Praying to Our Lord "paid off" for me, we might say. So I developed a habit of asking for favors, expecting to receive what I requested.

Being brought up in a Catholic environment makes it much easier to develop the habit of praying. Prayer offerings are the normal course of daily life. However, there are some dangers to this as well. Once you have acquired the habit of praying, it is easy to take saying prayers for granted, without giving them much thought. Prayers, we might say, become recited automatically, with little or no reflection on their words and meaning. The rote recitation of prayers can lead to your becoming distracted. You might slip easily into thinking about other daily activities, worries, or problems that need your attention. At the conclusion of your prayer, you might notice that you were hardly aware of what you were saying or why you were praying at all. While distractions can become problematic, don't let these discourage you or stop you from praying. Distractions are common, and you must persevere despite these. Your persistent effort, despite the distractions, will be pleasing to Our Lord.

Some people complain that saying prayers is "boring." They will use this as an excuse to avoid praying altogether. Ask yourself these questions before discontinuing your prayers: How would Our Lord respond to this excuse? What would He expect you to do if distraction becomes a problem? (Remember, the Father of Lies will jump for joy if he can tempt you to stop praying. Blaming prayers will be one of the tricks for luring you away from God.)

As noted earlier, when you enter secular society, you will be surrounded by people who, for the most part, pray very little. If you go to a restaurant to eat your lunch with secular friends, you will notice that few, if any of them, make the sign of the cross and say Grace before eating. At such a time, you will be tempted to omit the sign of the cross, and say Grace silently or not say it at all. Similar situations will arise when you attend social gatherings, at which food is offered. Ask yourself this question: How should I act when these circumstances arise? Think about this now. Don't get caught off guard — try to be prepared.

Unlike a Catholic environment, in which time is allotted for saying prayers throughout the course of the day, the secular world does not provide a daily schedule for praying. This responsibility will be up to you. Remember what I said about distractions? It will be easy to become distracted once you become burdened with the responsibilities of becoming an increasingly more independent adult. Ignoring, rushing, and eliminating prayers will be tempting, especially when you are feeling overwhelmed by obligations that demand your attention. Blaming prayers for being "boring" or just "the same old, same old" might seem to be reasonable excuses for cutting back or dropping your prayers altogether. Keep in mind that the Father of Lies would certainly support you in this line of reasoning.

As you make the transition into secular society, another problem with regard to the value of praying will arise. You will find that lots of people who once prayed faithfully no longer pray at all. They complain that prayers go unanswered no matter how much they pray. They blame God contending that He has a "deaf ear" and does not keep His promises. Like little children, they stomp their feet and pout. They fail to recognize that God always answers our prayers, but not in the way they expected. Remember how I prayed to God in my childhood years? I would bargain with Our Heavenly Father, hoping that He would honor my request, unconcerned about what He might have willed for me. As I matured, making childhood trades was no longer working. I had to find a more meaningful way to pray. Otherwise I too might stop praying.

My first step in the right direction occurred after reading the words of Saint Paul in his First Epistle to the Corinthians: "When I was a child, I spoke as a child; I understood as a child; I thought as a child. But when I became a man, I put away the things of a child…" After some reflection, I concluded that my past prayers were those of a spoiled child, rather than a Catholic adult who was committed to God and His Church.

Now that I was no longer a child, Our Lord expected me "to put away the things of a child" and to understand, speak, and act like an adult. This meant asking God for those things that are pleasing to Him and lead to the salvation of my soul. God has made it clear that all earthly trappings, if they were necessary in helping us to fulfill His Divine Plan, would be given to us as well. In light of this, Our Lord expects that we should have absolute trust in Him and remain stalwart in our Faith, especially when adversity arises.

A good example of the above appears in the Book of Kings. Most of you are familiar with the story of King Solomon. Because Solomon was a loving and loyal subject, God appeared to him in a dream and said, "Ask for whatever you want me to give you." Solomon answered, "So give your servant a discerning heart to govern your people and to distinguish between good and evil." Note that Solomon did not ask for a long life, honor, wealth, the death of his enemies, or any other temporal rewards. He asked for wisdom, not personal gain. Needless to say, God was pleased with Solomon's answer. He, therefore, not only endowed Solomon with wisdom, but promised him a long life, honor, wealth, and greatness, "that in your [King Solomon's] lifetime you will have no equal among kings." Obviously, King Solomon had "put away the things of a child" and behaved like a man of God.

The message of King Solomon is clear. It is up to us to determine that which is pleasing to God and request His help accordingly. Perhaps those things that we are requesting could be harmful to the salvation of our soul if God granted them. There is an old saying: "Be careful what you wish for—you just might get it." How many times do we hear about those rich and famous people who seem to have everything that life has to offer? Yet some of them ruin their lives and commit suicide. By appearing not to answer our prayers, Our Lord might be doing us a great favor. In our spiritual blindness, however, we whine like children, thinking that we know better than Him what is best for us. If you believe that Our Lord is not answering your prayers, then maybe some hard soul-searching is needed. Maybe that which you are requesting from God is not pleasing to Him. By denying your wish, He may be really answering your prayers. Think about this before you become tempted to stop praying. Remember the Father of Lies is lurking in the background patiently waiting for you to quit trying.

So the question arises: "What should I ask that would be pleasing to Our Lord?" Putting your absolute trust in Him would be a good place to start. After all, Our Lord emphatically stated the following (Saint Mark's Gospel, 11:22-24): "Have faith in God. Amen I say to you, whoever says to the mountain, 'Arise and hurl yourself into the sea' and does not waver in his heart, but believes that whatever he says will be done, it will be done for him. Therefore I say to you, all things whatever you ask for in prayer, believe that you shall receive, and they shall come to you."

In the above, Christ not only stresses the importance of a strong and unyielding Faith, but He asks you to "not waver in your heart" when you pray. Being persistent is emphasized here. If you become weak of heart, self-pity and despair can follow. It is at these moments that the devil will fill your head with irrational thoughts, encouraging you to give up praying altogether. Keep in mind that it is persistence, persistence, and more persistence which must not be overlooked. Again Our Lord emphasized the importance of this virtue in the Gospel of Saint Luke (11:5-13), as follows:

> [At that time, Jesus said to His disciples,] "Which of you will have a friend and shall go to him in the midst of the night and say to him 'Friend, lend me three loaves, for a friend of mine has come to me from a journey, and I have nothing to set before him.' And he from within should answer and say, 'Do not disturb me; the door is now shut, and my children are in bed; I cannot get up and give you anything.' I say to you although he

will not get up and give to him because he is his friend, yet because of his persistence, he will get up and give him all that he needs. And I say to you, ask and it shall be given to you; seek and you shall find; knock and it shall be opened to you. For everyone who asks receives; and he who seeks finds; and to him who knocks it shall be opened. But if one of you asks his father for a loaf, will he hand him a stone? Or for a fish, will hand him a serpent? Or if he asks for an egg, will he hand him a scorpion? Therefore, if you, evil as you are, know how to give good gifts to your children, how much more will your heavenly Father give the Good Spirit to those who ask him."

The unwavering practice of your Faith is what is pleasing to Our Lord. Putting total trust in Him is what He wants from you. This is the road leading to the answering of all of your prayers. When you have reached this goal, you will have "put away the things of a child" and "put on the things of a man." May God strengthen you in this endeavor.

To you, "the salt of the earth" and the light of the world," the prayer of Saint Ignatius of Loyola, asking for God's love and grace rather than earthly goods is offered: "Take, O Lord, and receive my entire liberty, my memory, my understanding, and my whole will. All that I have and possess You have given me. I surrender it all to be disposed of according to Your will. Give me only Your love and grace; with these I will be rich enough and desire nothing more."

On forming true friendships in a secular world

FROM: PAUL LAVIN, PH.D.

Dear Graduate,

Let me begin by saying that when you enter secular society, making true and lasting friendships will not be an easy task, particularly if you follow Christ's teachings. For instance, consider the Gospel of Saint Matthew (12:30), in which Our Lord emphatically stated, "He that is not with me is against me." Take a few seconds to think about the impact that this bold proclamation would have on those people who celebrate "tolerance" and "diversity" in our politically-correct society. Most likely they would bristle with indignation, claiming that such a statement borders on being prejudicial and intolerant of others.

As the preceding shows, Our Lord drew a clear line in the sand between Himself and His enemies. He intentionally polarized the world, placing its inhabitants in one of two camps. People were either with Him or against Him. He refused to allow them to take a "middle of the road" or what is called a "moderate" position. Our Lord forced them to choose sides. For them to claim that they were neutral was unacceptable.

In fact, throughout the Gospels Christ engaged in what modern man would call "extremist" or "black and white" thinking. He described the world as consisting of two kingdoms, Good versus Evil. These kingdoms were at constant war with each other—an ongoing battle between Our Lord and the Prince of Darkness, which would last until the end of time. Again, Our Lord insisted that we take sides in this battle. He never taught that neutrality or tolerating falsity were virtues. In fact Our Lord abhorred these. Note the following from Revelation, Chapter 3, verses 15-16: "I know your works; you are neither hot nor cold. Would you were hot or cold! So, because you are lukewarm I will spew you (vomit) out of my mouth." Notice that Our Lord did not mince His words, but spoke forthrightly on how He felt about those who would compromise His truth. The tone of His voice was militant. Our Lord did not beg or plead with us to become members of His Church. Rather, He commanded all of mankind to join with Him in the battle against Satan and his evil empire. No other choice is acceptable, if we want to save our souls.

Today's "moderates" would find Christ's words to be most disturbing. As noted earlier, they would accuse our Lord of being an "extremist" who was "black and white" in His thinking. They would further insist that the truth was neither black nor white but "gray," somewhere between these poles. Moreover, they would contend that the truth is still evolving. What is true today might change tomorrow. As you can see, the Catholic

Church, which openly proclaims that It is the only true Church, could easily arouse the ire of those who believe that one religion is just as good as another. Why? Because the Catholic Church contends that real truth lies only within Its teachings. All other churches are man-made institutions, which are flawed. This does not change with the times, even though modern man would like it to be so.

As a committed Catholic, you, like Our Lord, will be required to draw a line in the sand when it comes to the practicing of your Faith. There can be no compromise on the teachings of the Church on matters of faith and morals. You have been taught to believe that Christ the King should be the absolute ruler of mankind. The dogmas of His Church are etched in stone and must be followed at the peril of losing one's soul. Remember, Our Lord intends you to be "the salt of the earth" and "the light of the world" to shine for all to see, not hidden out of sight in an enclosed area. This is not an easy task when you enter the secular world. If you stand up for Christ and His Church, you can be reviled and mocked by your peers, professors, and other secular-thinking people with whom you associate.

Being treated disrespectfully can be painful, especially when it comes from those with whom you have formed close relationships. Close relationships are built on trust. Trust is based on the belief that your true friends not only understand you, but will be your advocate when others engage in gossip or make disparaging comments about your commitment to the Catholic Faith. Those who "sit on the fence," claiming that they are neutral and don't want to take sides, are false friends. They might not be critical when they are with you. However, when you are not with them, you can never be sure that they might not openly agree with your critics in private conversations. In other words, you cannot count on their loyalty, for them to "watch your back." And even if false friends say nothing, their silence can be interpreted as tacit approval of your adversaries' contentions.

False friends who fail to defend you or remain silent will provide you, a loyal practicing Catholic, with no solace when you are being tested. In fact, you are likely to feel betrayed, especially if you thought the person whom you trusted was a true friend—someone whom you could count upon to support you when you were surrounded by jackals, attacking the Faith and your commitment to it. Again, friends who sit on the fence, "playing both ends against the middle," proclaiming their neutrality, are acquaintances, not friends. Their neutrality actually strengthens those who are against and even hate the Church Militant.

Keep in mind that trust and the sharing of cherished beliefs are the foundation upon which true and enduring friendships are founded. In searching for friends, make sure that you take these into account. Ask yourself these questions before your friendship is formed: Is this a person with whom I can share my Catholic Faith? How would this person respond if Our Lord insisted that he or she choose to be with Him or against Him? Your honest answers to these simple questions will provide you with important information as to whether you wish to further pursue this relationship. Remember, true and enduring friendships are based on trust and those important principles that are held in common.

As a practicing Catholic, you must keep in mind that you will be vilified for thinking and acting as Christ intended. Aligning yourself with Him places you against Satan, the world, and those persons who are willing to compromise His Church and teachings. "He who is not with Me is against Me" is not an artificial distinction created by Our Lord to stir up controversy. Rather, it is a true depiction of reality, with which you must cope every day of your life. While you might not receive solace from fellow humans, Our Lord especially loves you, the "salt of the earth" and "the light of the world," who are ridiculed for His sake. Keep the Gospel of Saint Matthew (5:11-12) in mind when this happens: "Blessed are you when men reproach you, and persecute you, and speaking falsely, say all manner of evil against you, for my sake. Rejoice and exult because your reward is great in heaven." Hopefully, these words will buoy you up in times of trial.

May Almighty God give you, "salt of the earth" and "the light of the world," the wisdom to select true friends, who will stand with you in these times of trial.

On caution: beware of those who are Catholic in name only

FROM: PAUL LAVIN, PH.D.

Dear Graduate,

In my first Open Letter, I pointed out that many young Catholics discontinue practicing their Faith once they enter the secular world. Some will continue to call themselves Catholics. However, they are really Catholics-In-Name-Only.

Catholics-In-Name-Only, while professing to be Catholic, are far from being so. Typically, they pick and choose the teachings they decide to follow. The selection of what they choose to believe or reject is based on individual preference. Like their secular friends, Catholics-In-Name-Only reject the Church's dogmatic pronouncements, claiming that truth is still evolving. They, too, contend that what is true today might be false tomorrow.

Catholics-In-Name-Only would deny that Sunday Mass attendance is obligatory. Since the obligation to attend Mass on Sunday is not specifically stated in the Bible, they would insist that this proves their point. They would argue that this is a Church law made by men, not Jesus Christ. Where is it written that Our Lord said we had to attend Church on Sunday? they will ask.

The dogmatic pronouncement that "Outside the Catholic Church there is no salvation" would be viewed as uncharitable nonsense. The Catholic-In-Name-Only would insist that God is all-merciful. In order to be saved, what counts is being a "good person" who is sincere in his or her convictions.

Yet the reality is that everyone who attains salvation is saved through the Catholic Church. Needless to say, Catholics-In-Name-Only will differ with many, if not most, of the Church's teachings on faith and morals. They are unlikely to believe in the Real Presence of Our Lord's body and blood in the consecrated Eucharist. Like their Protestant friends, they will contend that the consecration is merely a reenactment of what occurred at the Last Supper. The Church's commandment requiring all Catholics to confess their sins and receive Holy Communion at least once a year—the fulfillment of our Easter Duty—will be rejected as well.

The infallibility of the pope, when he makes solemn declarations on faith and morals, has little or no impact on how Catholics-In-Name-Only conduct their lives. With regard to morals, they may hold firm to some of the Church's teachings, but reject others. For example, some Catholics-In-Name-Only might condemn abortion. However, on the other hand, they would support physician-assisted suicide. Again, the picking and choosing of what one considers to be moral or immoral is determined by each individual's preference. Following the Church's teachings on these matters is not obligatory.

For you, "the salt of the earth" and "the light of the world," Catholics-In-Name-Only can become a problem, particularly if you are attending a secular college or university. Catholics-In-Name-Only will misrepresent the true teachings of the Catholic Church. You, on occasion, may be called upon to correct these misrepresentations and to clarify and defend that which the Church really stands for. This will not be an easy task, especially if you are surrounded by Catholics-In-Name-Only who have twisted the Church's teachings to suit their own purposes. It might be of some help to know that Saint Paul, in his Second Epistle to Timothy (4:1-5), predicted such times and encouraged us to remain strong when such adversity arises. Saint Paul's Epistle is as follows:

> [Beloved:] I charge you in the sight of God and Jesus Christ, who will judge the living by his coming and by his kingdom, preach the word, be urgent in season, out of season; reprove, entreat, rebuke with all patience and teaching. For there will be a time when they will not endure the sound doctrine; but having itching ears, will heap up to themselves teachers according to their own lusts, and they will turn away from the truth and turn to fables. But be watchful in all things, bear with tribulations patiently, work as a preacher of the gospel, fulfill your ministry.

As you can see, Saint Paul's predictions, which occurred two thousand years ago, apply today.

He asks you, Our Lord's disciples in our modern world, to preach the true Catholic Faith to those who have been led astray. Saint Paul doesn't suggest that you aggressively attack those who have strayed from the truth. Rather, he asks you to be watchful, patient, and bear with tribulations. Patience will require that you pace yourself accordingly. Take the time to think and plan ahead. How might you best use your energy and ability when such occasions arise? How might you go about "fulfilling your ministry"? And lastly, how might Saint Paul's Epistle apply in your interactions with those who have become Catholics-In-Name-Only?

To you, "the salt of the earth," preserve your zest. Be patient and wisely use your energy and ability when adversity arises.

II

Open letters on the capital sins and temptation

On the capital sins and how the devil uses them

FROM: PAUL LAVIN, PH.D.

Dear Graduates,

n my previous Open Letters, I focused on many of the challenges you will encounter when you enter into the secular world. As I pointed out, you, "the salt of the earth" and "the light of the world," will be engaged in a life-long war with the Prince of Darkness. Your soul, whether it is lost or saved, will be determined by how well you wage this battle. In this Open Letter, the weaponry and nefarious tactics used by Satan to lure you away from Our Lord will be discussed.

As you know, sin and the various forms that this takes are the primary weapons that will be used against you. Before we discuss this further, however, let's review some of the key points on making the transition into secular society. First, remember that there is a devil, who is lurking in the shadows, waiting to tempt you. Don't ignore or under-rate him. The devil not only possesses superior intellectual powers, but he is a master of timing as well. He knows that you are currently residing in a Catholic environment, in which you are surrounded by prayer and the reception of the sacraments. Because you are well protected, the devil realizes that his diabolical tactics are less likely to be successful during this time of your life. While temptations will emerge from time to time, his best weaponry will be saved and used after you graduate. It is at that time, when you enter secular society, that you might be most vulnerable.

Remember, the devil knows your weaknesses. Equipped with this knowledge, he will try to devise a plan, especially designed for capturing your soul. There is an old saying, "One man's meat is another man's poison." This means that something who is viewed as being good by one person is considered to be bad by another. Satan is clever in this regard. He knows that which might be thought of as "meat" by you would be considered as being "poison" by your peers. So he customizes a plan filled with temptations that would appeal to you—not Harry, Tom, or Robert—but YOU. Take a few minutes to think about this. What are your weaknesses? What might the Father of Lies have in store for you when you enter the secular world?

In developing a plan to combat the devil, let's begin by looking at the Capital Sins, the primary weaponry that the Prince of the World will use in his effort to capture your soul. The seven Capital Sins, as you might recall, are: Pride, Greed, Lust, Anger, Gluttony, Envy, and Sloth. Why focus on the Capital Sins, you might ask? The answer to this question is simple enough. Capital Sins are the foundation from which all other sins arise. The devil is most likely to make good use of these in his attempts to entrap you.

It should be noted that of all the Capital Sins, Pride is the sin of sins—the grandfather of all sins we might say. It was Pride that toppled the devil from his exalted throne, and it was Pride that led to Adam and Eve's expulsion from the Garden of Eden. Hence, Pride is the original and most deadly of the Capital Sins.

Although Pride is the source of all sins, let's first focus on Envy. Envy is a Capital Sin that is closely aligned with Pride. Envy is the over-riding desire to possess the status, ability, or material goods belonging to other persons. Envious persons believe that others are more fortunate, smarter, popular, and more attractive than they are. Envy is dangerous. It can quickly lead to resentment, bitterness, and self-pity. Envy can become particularly problematic for those of you who will be associating with secular-thinking peers at the college or university that you are attending. This is why I chose to give this Capital Sin a top priority. Becoming envious of those who are successful in acquiring fame and fortune is a common human failing. Moreover, Envy can worsen when those who acquire these things taunt God's laws. This is particularly frustrating because it seems unfair, especially when you are young and life appears to be so promising.

Let's begin by looking at how the Father of Lies might tempt you into becoming envious of your peers. When you enter the secular world, you will meet a number of young people who are attractive, articulate, humorous, and self-confident. They will be sought after by others who want to be friends with them. These young, successful men and women will not only be looked up to by their peers, but will be admired by many adults as well. Some of them will be gifted in athletics, music, theatre, or in some other field. At a young age, they might acquire fame, wealth, and even local and national recognition because they are so talented.

You will notice that some of these gifted young people might openly and flagrantly violate God's laws and civil laws as well. Because they are talented and popular, however, they are able to avoid being punished for their wrongdoing. Living with a member of the opposite sex without being married, having children out-of-wedlock, drug and alcohol abuse, using foul language, blasphemy, and other sinful behavior might be overlooked or ignored by their peers and even adults who should know better. Despite their ongoing and brazen arrogance, you will notice that these youthful rebels continue to prosper. There seem to be no negative consequences attached to their obnoxious and sinful behavior. Rather, they remain popular and people continue to seek their approval and friendship. They seem to bask in being "bad," taunting God, the civil authorities, and others who try to live decent lives.

As pointed out previously, when you are young it is natural to want to have friends. You will want to be popular and to be viewed as being successful. You, like your peers, will want to be able to do those things other young men and women feel free to do. You will want to blend into your social surroundings—to fit in without having to be on guard and mistrusting of those people who think differently than you. If you choose to be a practicing Catholic, however, the latter is most likely to occur. Our Lord cautioned us about the danger involved in envying wrongdoers who seemingly prosper in this world. Moreover, He warned us that if we followed His teachings, we could expect to be scorned and persecuted. Read His words from the Gospel of Saint John (15:17-21).

> [At that time, Jesus said to His disciples,] "These things I command you that you may love one another. If the world hates you, know that it hated me before you. If you were of the world, the world would love what is its own. But because you are not of the world, therefore, the world hates you. Remember, the word that I have spoken to you. No servant is greater than his master. If they persecuted me, they will persecute you also. If they have kept my word, they will keep yours also. But all these things they will do to you for my name's sake because they do not know Him who sent me."

It is important to keep Christ's words in mind when you enter the secular world. Once this occurs, the Father of Lies will try to make you envious of those young people who appear to have unlimited freedom and seem to prosper even though they behave sinfully. Keep in mind that which was discussed previously. The Master of Deceit will tempt you by making evil appear to be much more attractive than it is. If you fall for this trick, like Adam and Eve, you will find that the so-called "good" fails to live up to that which was promised. Don't let the Father of False Promises corrupt you.

Remember, you are "the salt of the earth" and "the light of the world." Don't let the Capital Sin of Envy lure you away from Our Lord and His Church.

On pride, the father from which all sins arise

FROM: PAUL LAVIN, PH.D.

Dear Graduates,

n the last Open Letter, I pointed out that Pride is the source from which all other sins flow. You will recall it was Pride that caused Satan and Adam and Eve to fall from God's grace. Pride is the most malicious of the Capital Sins. Pride and arrogance go hand-in-hand. The proud man places himself above all men and God. Like Lucifer, he proclaims loudly, "I will not serve!" Today, more than ever, Pride has become a dominant force that is tearing away at the fabric of our society. Our arrogant and secular world no longer gives Christ the King the rudiments of recognition to which He is entitled. He is excluded from our public schools. He is ignored in our courts of law. And He and His Church are insulted and mocked by the media. Make no mistake about it! Pride is a subtle and dangerous sin that slowly and persistently eats away at the purity of your soul.

How does this happen, you might ask? Like all sins, Pride begins as something that appears to be good. Remember, we said that the devil makes things look better than they really are. Pride starts out as being called "self-respect." On the surface, "self-respect" is a good thing. God certainly intends that man should respect and love himself. Love and respect dignify our humanity. This is not sinful. However, when we glorify ourselves, placing ourselves above God and our fellow human beings, "self-respect" turns into Pride. Don't confuse self-glorification with "self-respect." The former arrogantly disregards God and our neighbor. Self-respecting persons, on the other hand, love God above all things, and they love their neighbors as themselves—the two greatest commandments given to us by our Lord.

In today's "all about me" society, self-respect has morphed into arrogant self-worship. This glorification of oneself is manifested in a number of ways. Decorating the body with multiple and elaborate tattoos; piercing and inserting bobbles and ornaments of various sorts into the flesh; dying the hair with bright colors; Mohawk hair-cuts; and outlandish grooming and clothing are just a few of the manifestations of self-glorification that have emerged over the past few decades. Interestingly, hand-held camera phones, which can be used to photograph yourself, have now become popular. Those photos, taken by your camera phone, are called "selfies." Selfies can then be forwarded to others in your social network. How much more self-centered can we become?

Sports reveal another area of Pride and arrogance. For example, football players, who successfully defeat an opponent, engage in taunting, finger-pointing, and silly end-zone dancing when they score a touchdown. This so-called "celebrating" is no more than a blatant insult aimed at their competitors. Head and chest banging, trash talk (the use of foul and insulting language), fist pumping, and facial distortions accompanied with a defiant YES! have gradually, over time, become acceptable behavior.

There are many people who will justify the preceding absurdities by arguing that "it's just part of the game." However, as a practicing Catholic you need to ask yourself these questions: Does this behavior add to or take away from "good sportsmanship," the foundation upon which competitive sports are supposed to be built? How does God view this behavior? What about our Blessed Mother? How does Our Lord view sports' commentators referring to a long pass as a "Hail Mary" or a spectacular catch as the "Immaculate Reception"? As a Catholic, you will need to honestly answer these questions. Will your flesh cringe the next time that a sports' commentator refers to a long pass as a "Hail Mary"? Or will you, like most mainstream Americans, "blow it off," claiming that it is "no big deal."

Unfortunately, pride extends far beyond our athletic fields. It has infested our academic institutions, business organizations, and our government as well. Our Lord warned us about those learned persons who become "puffed up" with their own self-importance, believing that they are more intelligent than others, and even God Himself. Because some people accumulate a wealth of worldly knowledge, it is easy for them to become intellectually arrogant. Laborers, policemen, firemen, restaurant employees, and those who work in the trades are looked down upon. Yet society could not function without the people who fill these essential jobs on a daily basis.

In today's society, attending a school of higher education and acquiring an advanced degree is often considered to be a necessity. Advanced degrees can certainly lead to better job opportunities. However, God never intended that everyone should be a college graduate. On the contrary! Our Lord distributed various talents to all members of the human race. If people develop their talents and use them as God intended, all of humanity would prosper. Status, money, and social pressure should not be reasons for attending a college or university.

Imagine a world populated only with office workers, planners, and intellectuals. In such a world, there would be no farm workers to cultivate the land and grow needed foods. There would be no truck drivers to deliver food to grocery stores. Even if food was available, there would be no one to pack and distribute it. There would be no transportation workers to drive buses and trains. As you can see, the whole social order would crumble. God has a plan for each one of us. No matter how important or unimportant this may seem, performing our job with excellence determines how well the whole of our society functions. Remember the perfectly-designed automobile that was described in the "Open Letter to Those Graduates Attending a Secular College or University"? What happened when the owner failed to properly care for it? How would this apply here? Think about the answers to these questions.

Keep in mind that God rewards those who follow His laws. He does not offer paradise to a person simply because one is more intelligent than another. Rather than "puffing ourselves up" in a quest to be better than others, it makes more sense to develop the talents that God has given to us. Remember, God is all-just. From those, to whom He has given great potential, He will require much. From those who are not as talented, He will require less. God has given talents to us so that we can be of service to Him and His people. The use that we have made of these talents will determine how we will be judged.

There is much more to be said about Pride and its negative impact on corporate America. Some corporate leaders, who should serve as inspirational role models to their employees, have been guilty of deceiving these workers. Leading business executives have been caught in what is called "cooking the books." This means they falsified the company's financial records so that the business appeared to be prospering. However, the facts indicated otherwise. This deception has allowed many of these executives to live lavishly, while their workers lost their jobs and were ruined financially. Their greed, which was fueled by the belief that they could successfully cheat the general public, is still having a negative impact upon our society.

Think about the preceding carefully. It is quite possible that a well-paying job might someday be offered to you. You might be asked to "cook the books," making alterations which misrepresent the truth. You might be assured by your boss and other executives that "this is the way business is done." You might be told that what you are being asked to do is a small indiscretion, nothing to worry about; "everybody does it" and "this is what you have to do to get ahead." Again, think about this now, before you find yourself caught in a web that will plague your conscience and ruin your reputation.

Lastly, let's examine Pride and politics and the effect that Pride has on the lives of an entire nation. Persons who are elected to public office have a great responsibility to God and those citizens whom they govern. It is important to keep in mind that it is God Who allows them to be placed in positions of great influence and power. Think about this key point. When Our Lord was taken to Pilate by the Jews, He told Pilate it was God Who allowed him to have power. Initially Our Lord did not answer Pilate's questions, which irritated Pilate. Finally, the following dialogue between Pilate and Our Lord occurred (John 19:10-11): Pilate therefore said to him, "Do you not speak to me? Do you not know that I have the power to release you?" Following these questions, Our Lord stated the following: "You would have no power at all over me were it not given from above."

As you can see, Christ clearly pointed out to Pilate that his political authority was given to him by God—not the Jews, Gentiles, the Roman army, or the citizens of Rome. Ultimately, it would be God, the highest Authority, to Whom Pilate would be accountable. In reading this portion of the Passion, notice Pilate did not want to condemn Jesus. Pilate was anxious about being caught in the position of having to do so. He appeared to be fearful, recognizing that Our Lord was not an ordinary man, but a king whose kingdom was not of this world.

Unlike Christ, however, Pilate was a politician. The problem facing him was two-fold. Pilate had to satisfy the Jews, who could cause political trouble for him in Rome. At the same time, Pilate's conscience was over-wrought with guilt because he knew he was condemning an innocent man. And how would you know that Pilate was fearful of condemning Christ? We simply have to look at how Pilate behaved. He tried to convince the Jews to release Christ, even offering to free Him instead of Barabbas. Eventually, Pilate recognized that there was no way to placate the Jews. He gave them permission to crucify Jesus. In order to try and free himself of guilt, Pilate then declared that Christ was innocent and openly washed his hands in an attempt to pacify his conscience. Deep down inside Pilate may have recognized that Jesus was the Son of God. In order to protect himself politically, however, he "passed the buck," preferring "to go along to get along," rather than do what was right.

As the preceding indicates, public servants are placed in hallowed positions by God. They, therefore, have the responsibility to acknowledge and follow His laws. Unfortunately, this responsibility is often ignored. Rather, today's politicians insist that God and His Church should be separated from the State. If God's laws happen to coincide with the laws of the State, the government will enforce them. But what should happen if the laws of the State are contrary to God's laws—for example, laws permitting abortion and same-sex marriage? What should we do then? What would Our Lord expect us to do? Would "washing our hands" in public and proclaiming our innocence be acceptable? Or how about proclaiming that the expression of religion is a "private matter," which should be kept to yourself, rather than openly discussed in a community forum? How would God expect you to deal with these issues when you enter secular society?

More than ever, politicians have become increasingly skilled in using clever language to avoid telling the truth. The word "spinning the truth" is part of the new language describing how this is done. For example, the word "misspoke" is now used instead of saying "I told a lie." "Collateral damage" is used to describe the death of innocent victims who are killed in a war. And "significant other" is used to identify boy and girl friends who have decided to openly live together without being married. As you can see, we have become quite skilled in twisting the truth to suit our own purposes. Remember the Father of Lies and how he tricked Eve? How would he respond if you told him that you "misspoke," after you gave in to one of his temptations?

As a young man or women who is about to enter secular society, you might plan to get a law degree and enter the field of politics and public service. Law and public service are noble callings, which require intelligence and high moral standards. If you decide to follow this path, you need to give serious thought about where you stand on issues that affect you as a practicing Catholic. What would God expect from you if you decided to run for public office? How would you deal with the issue regarding the separation of Church and State? Would you support same-sex marriage? Would you vote for abortion if the majority of persons in your district supported this position? Think about these issues now. It won't be long before you become a registered voter. You will be asked to vote for a candidate to represent you. Will you vote for politicians who support some good things, but are pro-abortionists? Will you use your Catholic Faith as a guide in casting your ballot? As a Catholic, it will be your responsibility to follow the laws of God as well as the laws of the State. What if State laws contradict God's laws? How will you cope with this?

You will have a lot to think about before you enter the secular world. Above all, be careful of the devil and his attempts to "puff you up" with arrogance and the false belief that God is not necessary in our attempts to build a more humane society. Worldly utopias cannot be built unless we have Christ the King to lead us. Unfortunately, we have failed to learn this important lesson.

You, "the salt of the earth" and "the light of the world": remember that Pride comes before the fall. Avoid becoming "puffed up" when you prosper, always exemplify the humility of Our Lord Jesus Christ.

On the capital sin of greed and the importance of charity

FROM: PAUL LAVIN, PH.D.

Dear Graduate,

Today's Open Letter discusses the Capital Sin of Greed. You will notice that Greed and Pride are "birds of a feather that flock together." In other words, Pride and Greed are similar in many ways. The excessive accumulation of worldly goods and the flagrant display of these are common to both Capital Sins.

Greed is a Capital Sin that develops slowly over time. Young people, like you, don't usually start out in life intending to be greedy. However, as you grow older, the attraction of money, power, and possessions can become increasingly more attractive than the pursuit of virtue. As a result, much more of your time and energy can become invested in the former rather than the latter.

Greed is the selfish desire for money, power, and possessions. Greedy people care little about the needs of others. They accumulate things for the pure pleasure of owning them. Oftentimes, they have no scruples about denying even the necessities to other people as long as they can "fatten their own nest." That's what birds of a feather do—they make sure that they accumulate as much wealth as possible, even if others unfairly suffer in the process.

Some of you might have read *A Christmas Carol* by Charles Dickens. The miserly old Scrooge in this story accumulated vast sums of money for its own sake. Scrooge claimed that "one is never rich enough" as a justification for his greedy behavior. Yet, even with all of his money, Scrooge was never content. The money languished in the safes of his counting house while squalor, poverty, and suffering were all around him. Being a shrewd and unprincipled business man enabled Scrooge to profit from the misfortune of others. As a young man, Scrooge hardly began his life intending to become an old miser. Like most young people, he was eager and idealistic. However, with the passing of time, his principles gradually fell by the wayside until personal gain became the only motive for conducting business. This is why you, "the salt of the earth" and "the light of the world," need to be careful about the Capital Sin of Greed. Like a cancerous tumor, it grows slowly and lethally until it squeezes the life out of the human body. The difference, however, is that Greed can squeeze the eternal life out of your soul.

The secular world which you will be entering is one that condemns Greed, at least on the surface. Yet in the secular world, the people who are idolized the most are those with vast amounts of money. The accumulation of wealth, in and of itself, is not evil. However, when money is accumulated for its own sake and used for excessive self-indulgence, the sin of Greed becomes a problem. Be alert as you grow older and prosper! The glitz and glamour of wealth can be very enticing. If you are not careful, it can lead you into thinking that you are better than other people. Comparisons regarding who has greater wealth can be turned into a game of social climbing. Each person tries to out-do the other. Weddings, birthday parties, and festive social gatherings can become a contest to see whose event will be the most elaborate. While charitable contributions might be made to worthy causes, these too can become a show of who is able to give or raise the most money.

Young people who are brought up in wealthy families can become jaded and materialistic if they are not careful. They can come to believe foolish things. For example, they might think that people who wear brand-name clothing and own the most up-to-date electronic devises are "cool." Those who can't afford these are then scorned and ridiculed. The seeds of social snobbery can be planted at an early age. Material possessions and their use can dominate your time and attention. The Father of Lies would certainly be happy with this line of thinking.

If you are currently in an all-encompassing Catholic environment, you will be protected from the above. Those of you, who attend parochial schools, might be required to follow a dress code or wear uniforms. This will lessen the temptation to focus on who does or does not wear brand-name clothing. Even more importantly, spiritual rather than materialistic values are emphasized both in and outside of the classroom. Hence, the likelihood of social snobbery is diminished.

As noted earlier, however, when you enter the secular world, this will change. If you want to be recognized as part of the "in-crowd," you will be expected to think and behave as they do. You too may be tempted to enter the contest of acquiring and lavishly displaying the things that you own. As you age in years, a bigger house, more money, better cars, expensive vacations, and possessing the best that money can buy can dominate all of your time and energy. If you find that you are beginning to follow this path, consider the warning given to His disciples by Our Lord in the Gospel of Saint Matthew (19:24): "It is easier for a camel to pass through the eye of a needle, than for a rich man to enter into the kingdom of heaven." How could this be, you might ask? The Gospel of Saint Luke (16:19-31), in which Our Lord tells the story of a rich man who accumulated great wealth and lived a self-indulgent life, can help you to answer this question. The Gospel is as follows:

> [At that time, Jesus said to the Pharisees,] "There was a certain rich man who used to clothe himself in purple and fine linen, and who feasted every day in splendid fashion. And there was a certain poor man named Lazarus who lay at his gate, covered with sores, and longing to be filled with the crumbs that fell from the rich man's table;

even the dogs would come and lick his sores. And it came to pass that the poor man died and was borne away by the angels into Abraham's bosom; but the rich man also died and was buried in hell. And lifting up his eyes, being in torments, he saw Abraham from afar off and Lazarus in his bosom. And he cried out and said, 'Father Abraham, have pity on me, and send Lazarus to dip the tip of his finger in water and cool my tongue, for I am tormented in this flame.' But Abraham said to him, 'Son, remember you that in your lifetime have received good things, and Lazarus in like manner evil things; but now here he is comforted whereas you are tormented. And beside all that, between us and you a great gulf is fixed, so that they who wish to pass over from this side to you cannot, and they cannot pass from your side to us.' And he said, 'Then father, I beseech you to send him to my father's house, for I have five brothers, that he may testify to them lest they too come into this place of torment.' And Abraham said to him, 'They have Moses, and the Prophets, let them hearken to them.' But he answered, 'No, father Abraham, but if someone from the dead goes to them, they will repent.' But he said to him, 'If they do not hearken to Moses or the Prophets, they will not believe even if someone comes from the dead.'"

As you can see, the rich man was a person of great wealth who lived lavishly. He basked in luxury, while Lazarus, who was right outside of the gate, was ignored and suffered greatly. The rich man didn't beat Lazarus or treat him cruelly. Rather, he took no notice of Lazarus, filling each day with self-indulgent pleasures. The rich man's lack of charity and his pleasure-seeking corrupted him. This led to his eternal damnation. Unfortunately, the rich man became so self-absorbed and spiritually dulled that he was hardly aware of the misery and poverty of those around him. For this negligence, he was sent to Hell. Obviously, the rich man regretted being so uncharitable. However, once he died, it was too late to make amends.

The importance of behaving charitably toward our neighbor is stressed repeatedly by Our Lord and the Apostles. For example, consider the Epistle of Saint Paul to the Romans (13:8-10), which is as follows:

> [Brethren:] "Owe no man anything except to love one another: for he who loves his neighbor has fulfilled the Law. For 'You shall not commit adultery. You shall not kill. You shall not steal. You shall bear false witness. You shall not covet.' And if there be any other commandment, it is summed up in this saying, 'You shall love your neighbor as yourself.' Love does no evil to a neighbor. Love therefore is the fulfillment of the Law."

There is an old saying that applies to those people who are exceedingly conscientious about being high up on the social ladder. It is called "keeping up with the Joneses." This means that if your neighbor purchases something, then in order to measure up to him, you too should be able to purchase that item. As you can see, this can become a never-ending contest. And this only worsens, if you believe that you must surpass the wealth of others. As you age, be on guard. Don't let Greed get the best of you. Remember the Gospel story of the rich man and Our Lord's warning about the acquisition of material possessions. These will be of no value to us when we stand before Him to be judged. Loving our neighbor as ourselves and behaving charitably toward him, however, can earn merit for us. It is this merit—our acts of kindness—that can lead us to the most important possession of all—the Beatific Vision of Our Lord in Heaven.

For you, "the salt of the earth" and "the light of the world": be an example of charity, loving your neighbor as yourself.

On the capital sin of anger and how this can lead to hate and revenge

FROM: PAUL LAVIN, PH.D.

Dear Graduate,

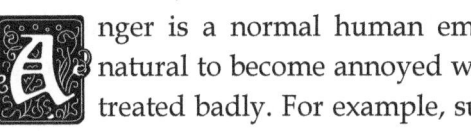nger is a normal human emotion. It is natural to become annoyed when we are treated badly. For example, suppose you were driving your automobile and another motorist rushed through a stop sign, nearly running into you. It is normal to become angry. After all, the other driver not only failed to stop, but he could have caused a serious accident. The anger that you feel at that moment is not a Capital Sin. It is an ordinary emotional reaction to another person's careless behavior.

However, let's take this one step further. Suppose that you started thinking about the other driver and began ruminating about his carelessness. Thoughts such as, "Where is a cop when you need him," and, "That jerk shouldn't be allowed to drive," run like wildfire through your mind. Your anger now turns into what is currently called "road rage." You then accelerate the speed of your car and begin chasing him. You scream obscenities through an open window, and try to run his automobile off of the road. Obviously, you are losing all emotional control. Unless right reasoning is restored, you could be in serious trouble. Your anger has turned into wrath, compounded by the wish to do evil to the driver who nearly caused an accident. It is at this point that your anger could become a Capital Sin. Hate and a thirst for revenge would be motivating your actions.

In today's world, the general public is pummeled with violent video games and movies. The male and female heroes in these movies wreak havoc on dictators, armies, and organizations that are evil. Using violent means, these superheroes demolish the evildoers. For ordinary folks, seeing these villains get what they deserve can be gratifying.

A good example of the preceding occurred in a series of movies a few decades ago. The titles were *Death Wish 1, 2,* and *3* starring Charles Bronson. You might have seen these movies. They are still shown and continue to be quite popular. The main character, Paul Kersey, was presented as an ordinary man who worked as an architect. Paul loved his family and was highly respected in his community. During the course of the story, several young thugs broke into Paul's home. They terrorized his family, and murdered them. Naturally, Paul was justifiably angry. The police conducted their investigation, but no suspects were identified and no leads were found.

Meanwhile Paul became increasingly impatient with the criminal justice system. This impatience eventually escalated into wrath. He then decided to take matters into his own hands. Paul systematically identified and hunted down each of the thugs and executed them. Moreover, in the process of obtaining his revenge, he killed several other muggers who were harassing innocent people. To the general public, Paul became a hero known as the Vigilante. Unlike the ineffective police department, Paul succeeded where the law had failed.

Who among us would not be tempted to take the law into our own hands if we were Paul Kersey? But the question that arises is this: Did Paul have the moral right to judge and execute these men even though they might be considered "the scum of the earth" by civil society? Paul Kersey was an intelligent, rational human being. However, the *Death Wish* for revenge led him into murdering those thugs who terrorized his family. But, we might say, the police had been ineffective in bringing these evil men to justice. Wouldn't this justify Paul's behavior?

As ordinary human beings, it is natural to experience a feeling of satisfaction when the so-called "scum of the earth" get what we think they deserve. But as practicing Catholics, how would God expect us to view Paul Kersey's quest for vengeance? Remember, Our Lord instructed us to forgive and behave charitably toward our enemies. Saint Paul, in his Epistle to the Romans (12:19-21) stated it is written that "Vengeance is mine. I will repay says the Lord." Saint Paul points out that by treating our enemy with forgiveness and charity, we would be heaping "hot coals of fire upon his head." What do you think Saint Paul meant by these words?

A point to keep in mind is that the number of movies like *Death Wish* are commonplace today. Superheroes wreak havoc on powerful individuals and evil organizations that trample on the rights of weaker people who cannot fight back. What makes the evildoers hated even more is that they show no remorse for their wrongdoing. And to make matters worse, they often take great pleasure in inflicting suffering on others. Who among us would not feel a sense of gratification when some superhero inflicts "pay-back" on these villains?

Keep in mind, however, that Hollywood producers recognize that movies like *Death Wish* attract the public, and are profitable as well. Hence, many movies are produced which appeal to the sinful side of our human nature. The infliction of revenge on evildoers is a theme which can make big bucks at the box office.

Violent movies seem to be everywhere. They appear on television, movie theaters, and can be purchased and played at home. While they are entertaining and seem to be harmless, the messages they convey can slowly influence our thinking and behavior. The heroes who entertain us may be overly angry and vengeful. Because they are stronger than their hated adversaries, however, this is ignored or overlooked. The overwhelming use of force, in which the good guys crush the evildoers, is a popular scenario. They don't have to rely on a slower-moving justice system or deal with the legal complications of a court trial. They don't have to think of criminals as human beings who, despite their wrongdoing, are loved by Jesus Christ. Moreover, they don't have to think about forgiveness and charity, especially when it concerns the so-called "scum" who inflicted suffering on innocent victims. A question that we need to ask is this: What might we have done to help this sick soul become a loved, rather than hated, member of society? The rousing of hatred, wrath, fury, and rage in response to injustice can be powerfully appealing, particularly when it appears in a movie. However, in real life, those of us who succumb to this may become spiritually dull in the process.

Being a Catholic is not easy. Stop and ask yourself about the movies that you watch and the messages they convey. Again some questions arise: Should you be watching these movies at all? And if you do watch them, how do they affect you? Do those human beings who do evil have an immortal soul? Should they be destroyed like wild animals?

But the big question is this: How would Our Lord view these Hollywood films? How would He expect you to cope with evildoers, especially if their actions impacted you and your family? Are your answers to these questions reflective of your Catholic Faith? Or would they be more in-line with the world in which we live? Don't let Hollywood movie producers do your thinking for you. It's up to you to decide!

You, "the salt of the earth" and "the light of the world": forgive and behave charitably toward your enemies. Trust that Our Lord will judge those who do you harm and generously reward you for putting your absolute confidence in Him.

On the capital sin of gluttony—"getting wasted"

FROM: PAUL LAVIN, PH.D.

Dear Graduate,

luttony is a Capital Sin, which is so common that it is hardly ever noticed. Although we are becoming a nation of obese people, we make all kinds of excuses to justify eating to excess. The genetic makeup that we inherited from our parents and grandparents is often cited as the cause for obesity. Blaming our inherited genes makes it easier to avoid taking responsibility for the consequences of gluttonous habits. It supports the notion that obesity is a fixed, unchangeable trait. There is, therefore, nothing or little that can be done about it. Rather than self-control, the easiest road to follow is to let nature run its course. If weight gain occurs, buy larger, loose fitting clothing and adjust to your expanding girth.

The problem with gluttony is that it not only involves overeating, but it might be accompanied by smoking and drinking to excess as well. The main source of these self-indulgent habits is the pursuit of gratifying the sense of taste. With regard to food particularly, the temptation to engage in gluttony is all around us.

God certainly intended that human beings should experience pleasure from eating. Without such pleasure, who among us would take the time and effort necessary to nurture and sustain a healthy body? God, in His infinite wisdom, constructed man with this in mind. Moreover, He certainly expected that tasteful, nutritious, and healthy food consumption should occur in a mannerly fashion within reasonable boundaries. In other words, the human person should not only properly regulate how much he eats, but should consume his food in a civil way as well. It is the civil consumption of food that distinguishes us from the beasts of the earth. In this regard, God expects us to treat and eat our food far differently than animals. God has given us the power to reason, and He intends for us to exercise this accordingly. The failure to regulate our eating habits not only defies our human nature, but leads to serious sinful behavior as well. Man's instincts are controlled by his will. Unlike a dog that eats when it smells food, a man eats when he wants to — unless he acts like a dog.

The secular world, while giving lip service to the above, seldom encourages that which God intended. Rather than focusing on healthy and dignified eating habits, the media bombards our senses with pictures of artificially created non-nutritional foods such as candy, chips, pastries, and sugar-laden, heavily-seasoned products of various sorts. Unreasonably large portions of meat and vegetables laced with dressings, spices, and sauces are displayed. The added condiments enhance the flavor of the food and appeal to our animal instincts. The sights, sounds, and projected smells emitted by these images stimulate the palate and intensify the sensual enhancement associated with eating. If we are not careful, such excitation can encourage overeating and even gorging ourselves to the point of nausea.

Today we hear jokes about how many Americans have become "couch potatoes." This is not really a laughing matter. How often do we see a group of mindless men—couch potatoes—sitting around a television set watching a football game. Not only are they sloppily dressed and poorly groomed, but their ridiculous behavior is often the equivalent of a six- or seven-year-old child. At the same time, these mindless "couch potatoes" spend their time gorging on chips, dip, and other "junk foods," which are spread out on a large table. Note that these are called "junk foods" for a reason. They lack any nutritious value and may actually be harmful to the body. The "junks foods" are often washed down with drinks, which also have no nutritional value. These beverages also contain alcohol.

The audience is encouraged to view the preceding as normal "mainstream" behavior. The riotous and happy crowd shows no restraint. Like animals, they satiate their carnal appetites until they are "wasted." Wasted is a substitute word for being drunk or intoxicated. As far as the advertisers are concerned, drinking to excess is "no big deal," provided that you make the proper preparations beforehand. You are encouraged "to drink responsibly." This means appointing a friend as "the designated driver" — someone who agrees not to drink and who will transport drunken friends to their homes. As you can see, such a situation can quickly become gluttonous. Again, this is common today. We seldom stop to think about it. Rather, overeating, gorging, and drinking to excess have become a national pastime.

Think about the real purpose of those advertisers who promote the sale of "junk foods" and intoxicating beverages. Ask yourself why they make gluttony so attractive. Their real purpose is to make money. Again, think about this carefully. The greater the food and alcohol consumption, the better profit these companies make. Suppose the general public changed their eating habits so that they consumed food and beverages that were healthy for the body. Suppose people decided to eat and drink only in moderation, and avoided those foods that were filled with chemicals, preservatives, and other artificial substances. What would happen to the companies' profits? What changes would they have to make if they wanted to stay in business?

How often do we stop to think about the Capital Sin of Gluttony and the many bad habits associated with it? We are surrounded with tables filled with food, which is picked over, pushed aside, falling onto the floor, partly eaten, and carelessly thrown into a trash bin. Think about the large number of people who are constantly hungry. Many would fight with each other to eat the scraps that are thrown into the trash. Remember the story that Our Lord told about Lazarus and the rich man, and how Lazarus was so poor he longed to eat the crumbs that fell from the rich man's table? Gluttony can blind us to the suffering of our fellow human beings. These starving people hardly worry about becoming obese or being placed in a weight loss program.

Again, as Catholics who will be entering the secular world, the time to think about these issues is now, before you face these problems firsthand. What do you suppose Our Lord thinks about the foods that we eat and the manner in which we consume them? Would Our Lord accept an invitation to an "all-you-can-eat buffet"? And if He did, how would He conduct Himself? Ask yourself these questions before you engage in your next "eat-a-thon." While the world will tell you that "it's no big deal" and "everybody does it," would these be satisfactory answers from Our Lord's point of view? Or would He expect us to conduct ourselves differently and set a better example?

The following might better demonstrate the seriousness of gluttony and our blind acceptance of it. Most of you are aware of the various eating contests, in which participants attempt to consume as many hot dogs, oysters, pies, ice cream, or other foods within a specified time limit. The winning competitor is lauded and receives a cash reward for his gluttony. Not so long ago a hot dog eating contest was sponsored on national television. Observation of this event showed how disgusting gluttony can be. The participants did not actually eat the hot dogs. Rather, they stuffed them into their mouth, barely chewed them, and swallowed the hot dogs almost whole. The competitors were not only required to eat the hot dogs, but they were instructed not to vomit or they would be disqualified. One of the participants even admitted that he swallowed his own vomit to prevent this from happening. Keep in mind that the participants not only appeared on national television, but were applauded for their gluttonous behavior. Vice became a virtue, not a Capital Sin, which was in violation of God's law.

As a practicing Catholic, you must ask yourself how God views these eating contests. What does He think about those who sponsor and participate in these events? You can see that gluttony can occur in many different settings. It not only happens at dinner parties, sporting events, and other social gatherings. Some businesses sponsor and encourage gluttony, and handsomely reward those who willfully and gleefully participate in it.

Lastly, some of your friends might claim that they enjoy the taste of alcohol. However, the large majority of young people who drink do so for the express purpose of getting "wasted." They often illegally purchase alcoholic beverages, store them in a private place, and pick a specific time and place for their consumption. The seriousness of this behavior should not be overlooked. Because they intentionally choose to become intoxicated, these young people are committing a mortal sin, which is the ultimate insult to God and His authority. They relinquish their free will; their higher faculties become dulled; they behave irrationally. No person in their right frame of mind, would want to stand before God in a drunken condition, attempting to plea for the salvation of his soul.

There are some practical problems that you should consider before allowing yourself to become "wasted." Once you are intoxicated your inhibitions will be lowered. This can quickly result in doing or saying things that you would never allow to happen when you are in a state of sobriety. Because alcohol can impair your ability to reason, you are unlikely to recognize that you may be behaving foolishly. The things that you say and do cannot be taken back or simply forgotten with the passage of time. In fact, in our current age of electronic gadgets, someone might use a handheld device to record your outlandish behavior, making you even more vulnerable. Think about these consequences, which could ruin your reputation. How might your family be affected by your actions? What would happen if you were arrested for under-age drinking? What if you were involved with a group that destroyed property or engaged in a conflict with the police? Could you be expelled from school and how would this affect your future? How would you feel if you became so inebriated that you lost your memory and self-control? And how would you feel if someone videotaped your behavior and showed it to others?

These are just a few of the complications that can occur when you engage in impulsive, careless drinking. Stop and think of this temptation now, before you attend your first social gathering at which alcoholic beverages are made available to you. All forms of gluttony will have a negative impact on your relationship with God. It can also permanently damage your future and seriously undermine the trusting bond between you and your family. Don't be so foolish as to think that this could not happen to you.

To "the salt of the earth" and "the light of the world": be temperate in your eating and drinking habits, exemplifying the teaching of Our Lord, Jesus Christ. Remember, you are a disciple of the young people of your generation, representing Him and His Church here on earth.

On the capital sin of sloth and the danger of becoming spiritually slothful

FROM: PAUL LAVIN, PH.D.

Dear Graduate,

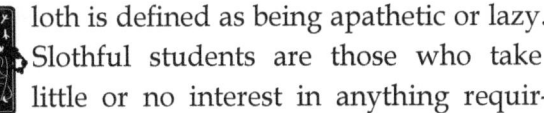loth is defined as being apathetic or lazy. Slothful students are those who take little or no interest in anything requiring serious effort and hard work. They are often self-indulgent and put off the completion of difficult tasks. The bulk of their time is spent in watching television, playing video games, and engaging in activities that they enjoy. More important tasks, such as school work and the completion of chores around the home, are neglected. Even if these tasks are completed, they are done so poorly that it would have been better if they had not been attempted at all.

Students who are held accountable for behaving responsibly are less likely to be slothful. Parents and teachers, who encourage and reward responsible behavior, usually produce highly-motivated students with good work habits. Proper character training helps young people, like you, to learn and acquire the emotional strength to cope with life's challenges. Self-disciplined students are able to concentrate and complete difficult, boring, and repetitive tasks, which overwhelm those who become easily distracted. Try to discipline yourself. Concentrate and be persistent! Make yourself do that which is difficult. Don't let the Capital Sin of Sloth interfere with your opportunity to be successful.

An athlete who must train in order to win a contest is a good example of the above. The athlete's goal is to win the contest. Winning the contest will not be easy, however. The actual training for the event will require much hard work and persistence, which might have to be stretched over a long period of time. Strenuous training is an arduous ordeal. But the training is necessary in order for the athlete to attain his goal. The highly-motivated athlete knows that he must discipline himself in order to perform to the best of his ability. He makes himself do the needed hard work that will significantly improve his chance of winning the contest.

The slothful athlete, on the other hand, views the situation differently. He would like to win the contest, but he lacks the desire and determination to train for the event. The inability to discipline himself will most likely cause him to fail. This failure will occur not because he lacks the potential to be victorious. Rather, his apathy and laziness will keep him from achieving his goal. Hence, the slothful athlete's character weakness, not his God-given ability, would be the cause of his failed performance.

When you graduate, most of you will have developed those work habits needed for success in the secular world. The people around you will encourage and reward your good work habits. You will be encouraged and rewarded for the development of musical, artistic, and athletic talents and for participating in charitable programs that help the less fortunate. Such recognition and support makes it less likely that you will be slothful. Rather, you will be highly motivated. Developing and using your talents is not only good for you, but this benefits secular society as well. By supporting you, secular society will profit from your efforts. Even Our Lord acknowledged that the world takes care of its own. Once you enter the secular world, you will understand what He meant by this.

It is spiritual sloth that might become the demon taunting you once you leave your family, school, and local community. As pointed out previously, you currently reside in a Catholic environment, in which prayer and the sacraments are readily available to you. Moreover, you are constantly encouraged and praised for being a faithful Catholic. It is this that is most likely to change when you enter secular society. If you attend a secular college or university, the frequent reception of the sacraments may not be readily available. Attending Mass, frequent Confession, and saying daily prayers might become burdensome rather than a source of spiritual satisfaction. You might find that your time is now becoming filled with studies, organizational affiliations, athletics, and other social events. You might ask yourself this question: Who really cares whether I go to Mass, receive the sacraments, or pray?

Unlike your pre-graduation days, there may be no adults or friends who care about the Catholic Church. For them, religion may not be important. In such circumstances, it will be tempting to become spiritually lax. There may be little or no support for practicing the Faith. Some people might even look down on you, believing that religion, particularly the Catholic religion, is a waste of time and effort. As noted earlier, it is much easier to be a devout Catholic when your home, school, and the community share the same beliefs. When you enter secular society, this will not be the case. Whether you attend an institution of higher learning, a trade school, enter the work force, or join the military, the challenges to continue practicing the Faith will be plentiful. The question that will arise is: What should you do when these challenges arise? This is an area in which the secular world will test you. Will you be ready when this battle begins?

There are also some other difficult questions that you will need to address in preparation for what is to come. What signs might be a warning that you are becoming spiritually slothful? What steps must you take if such laxity begins to occur? What must you do to make sure that you attend Mass and receive the sacraments? How should you arrange your schedule so that the practice of your Catholic Faith continues to be the top priority in your life?

With regard to the last question, the practice of your Faith is expected to be your number one priority. This was made clear by Our Lord when He gave us the greatest commandment in the Gospel of Saint Mark (12:30): "Thou shall love the Lord thy God with thy whole heart, thy whole soul, and with thy whole mind, and with thy whole strength." Keep in mind that this is not what the devil wants you to hear and believe. Don't let him lull you into spiritual laxity. This will be one of the many deceptions that he will try to use to capture your soul.

You are "the salt of the earth." Don't lose your strength. Continue to add zest to the world by your example. You are "the light of the world." Continue to shine where you can be seen by all men.

On the capital sin of lust—the devil's favorite weapon

FROM: PAUL LAVIN, PH.D.

Dear Graduate,

s you know, all Capital Sins can be destructive. However, Lust is the Capital Sin which the devil relies on most readily to capture souls, particularly the souls of innocent young people. In fact, our Blessed Mother told Lucia, Francisco, and Jacinta, the seers of Fatima, that "sins of the flesh" would lead to the damnation of the large majority of people.

Make no mistake about it! Lust, the passionate arousal of sexual desire, is very intense. Once aroused, Lust becomes extremely difficult to overcome. This is why Lust is a favored weapon used by the devil. Teenagers, young adults, and even older people can easily be drawn into the devil's seemingly harmless, pleasure-promising trap. With regard to adults, this partly explains why there are so many divorces. Once their unchaste desire is satisfied with one partner, they move on to another. The Sacrament of Marriage given to us by Our Lord becomes a mockery. While re-marrying is legal in the eyes of the State, such unions are viewed as being sinful by God and His Church.

Again, the devil makes sin appear to be both harmless and attractive. However, once your soul becomes corrupted, you will find that Satan's false promises fall far short of your expectations. Regret is soon to follow. Keep in mind that Lust is one of the devil's favorite sins. He can make it appeal to almost everyone, especially those who do not pray for the strength to overcome its powerful allure.

Most people seem to be unaware of the dominant place that Lust has taken in our television shows, movies, advertisements, fashions, music, and other facets of society. Satan uses those who control the media to promote Lust and to sell his lies to a naïve and unsuspecting public. The media has increasingly bombarded the general public with immodest and impure material for the last several decades. As a result, they have become desensitized as to how serious the problem has become. Young people would deny being negatively influenced by this bombardment. However, this is far from the truth. Don't let this happen to you. Be aware. Take our Blessed Mother's warning about the dangers of Lust seriously. Otherwise, like many other unsuspecting souls, you too will be tricked by the Father of Lies.

Again, keep in mind that most people fail to see through the subtle and steady stream of impurity thrust upon us by the media. They have become so dulled to the presence of Lust that they are unprepared, just waiting to be tempted. Recognizing their vulnerability, Satan floods their lower appetite with attractive sensual lures. Once aroused, these become most difficult to resist.

In order to protect yourself, it is important that you be aware of those daily influences promoting Lust. The psychological trickery used to deceive you and what you can do to avoid Satan's traps also need to be addressed. Watch out for the deceptive language used by the media, untrustworthy peers and adults, and society itself. Keep in mind that the tricky use of words is designed to weaken your resistance and corrupt you.

The rest of this Open Letter will focus on those industries, businesses, and people promoting Lust and how they will try to influence you. Because there is so much material to cover, this Open Letter will be much longer than usual. In order to make the contents easier to read and understand, subtitles are used to identify each topic to be discussed. These subtitles and their order of presentation are as follows: 1. Advertising; 2. Television; 3. Movies; 4. Music; 5. Peers; 6. Society; 7. Fashions; 8. Adult Role Models; and 9. Consequences of Lust. Let's begin by focusing on Advertising, the first topic, which is as follows.

1. Advertising

Advertising appears in all forms of the media. Ads are often designed with the intent of arousing lustful feelings within the viewer. For example, advertisers pay models, particularly female models, to dress in scanty, immodest clothing.

Advertisers know that these attractive women can quickly arouse sexual feelings in those males who are viewing them. Advertisers want you, the potential customer, to associate these pleasurable feelings with their product. In this way, they hope to entice you to purchase whatever they happen to be selling.

God created sexual feelings. He intended that these be expressed only between married people. To willfully think about or express these feelings outside of the marital state is sinful. Attraction to the opposite sex is natural. However, it was never God's intent that this should be used for business purposes.

At this point you might ask, "Does this approach to advertising work in selling products?" The answer is obvious: "Yes, it works." Keep in mind that business people are not foolish. They would not spend money on ads unless these led to increasing sales. Since these ads are so common, we would have to assume they make money for the businesses that use them. Although these ads are offensive to God, this is not taken into consideration. Again, businesses use this approach because it makes large sums of money. Some advertisers would justify this by saying, "That (making money) is the bottom line and that is why we are in business." How do you think God would respond to this rationalization? Does the end (making money) justify the means (the arousal of lustful desire)? What is wrong with this line of reasoning?

As the preceding indicates, the lustful use of sex in advertising is morally wrong. Because such advertising has become so common, however, we have become insensitive to this. We have forgotten that the expression of sexual feelings should only occur between a man and a woman who are validly married in the eyes of God. If we fail to keep this in mind, we will become careless and think of sexual expression as a recreational activity. Such thinking is grossly offensive to Our Lord and what He intended.

Keep in mind that the frequent viewing of impure commercials can have a dulling effect on you. Like many of those in the secular world, you too can become overly casual about the expression of sexual feelings. Remember, commercials are designed to help businesses to make money, even if this is at the expense of your purity. Sexual expression is not the plaything that the media presents it to be. Guard your eyes and ears from impure things.

2. Television

As noted previously, advertisers are guilty of disregarding God's plan for the proper expression of sexual feelings. Television shows, particularly situational comedies called sitcoms, are guilty of this as well. The characters in situational comedies are often attractive. Their grooming, dress, and other attire are usually in style or "cool." They are outgoing, energetic, and funny. Because they are young and popular, they are viewed as role models, the kind of people we would like to be.

Because sitcom characters have many positive qualities, you can, without realizing it, become heavily influenced by them. You can, if you are not careful, begin thinking the way they think; talking the way they talk; and acting the way they act. This can become particularly dangerous when it comes to forming your attitudes about the proper expression of sexual feelings and how this relates to God's plan. Again, the expression of sexual feelings is reserved only for married men and women. Sexual thoughts and behavior outside of the marital state are violations of God's commandments. The expression of sexual feelings is not a joke to be taken lightly. It is part of God's plan for the creation of human life. Sitcom programs and characters seldom treat this accordingly.

Sitcom characters often make jokes about sex and its expression. While these jokes lead to much laughter, they unfortunately convey the notion that sex is not a serious topic. Rather, it is portrayed as being humorous. Some would say, "It's no big deal." You need to be on guard so that you don't become influenced by these insensitive, careless portrayals. If you are not careful, you, like many sitcom characters, will grossly under-rate the seriousness and sacredness of what God intended.

Unfortunately, much of a thirty-minute sitcom program is filled with shallow, careless interpersonal encounters. These encounters are an insult to God and his plan for the procreation of the human race. They largely focus on sexual impulses and the physical attraction surrounding this. Sexual expression is presented as a harmless, playful activity. Wouldn't the devil want you to view it in this way? Think back on our discussion of the Father of Lies and how he can lure you into damnation.

Again, taking sexual expression lightly can be dangerous. In today's world, it is easy to become short-sighted. Viewing television programs can take up a good part of your daily activities. Television programs can have a powerful impact on the way you think, feel, and act. It's up to you to make sure that you, not the television programs and characters, control your thinking and behavior. Don't lose sight of God's plan in a world that has become obsessed with Lust. Don't laugh at sexual jokes, even if other people are doing so. Keep in mind that even if you are an inactive participant, your willful listening and attention can be interpreted as approval.

3. Movies

Television certainly can influence the way we think and act. However, movies can be even more powerful in influencing our attitudes on human sexuality. Over the past half-century, movies have changed significantly. The use of foul language, rude behavior, intense violence, and graphic cruelty are commonly presented. Moreover, nudity and sexual activity are now vividly portrayed on the screen. Little, if anything, is left to your imagination. You have to think carefully about what you watch so that you don't become overly influenced by it. Keep in mind that movies run for about two hours. Movies often take important topics, situations, and human relationships and present them in a sequence of scenes. Each scene lasts for a short period of time. The movie shifts from one scene to another, which might involve the same or new people in different situations. These brief encounters are hardly a complete or true depiction of reality.

Keep in mind that movie producers are not interested in educating you about the proper expression of sexual feelings and God's plan regarding this. They put graphic sexual scenes into the movies because they believe that the general public finds these to be entertaining. Entertaining movies that highlight Lust make money for the movie producers.

There are some things that you need to think about. Movies frequently portray two adults who, after a brief encounter, become physically attracted to each other. This may be followed by a short courtship and the consensual agreement to engage in lustful activity. Such scenes are certainly offensive to Our Lord. They seldom, if ever, focus on the importance of marriage and the responsibilities that a husband and wife have toward each other in cooperating with God's plan.

Again, like television sitcoms, the sexual scenes in movies are often humorous and playful.

Because two consenting adults are involved, it is easy for you to conclude that lustful behavior is acceptable and harmless. If you see adults behaving in this way, why should a young person, like yourself, not do the same? Once more a word of caution is in order. Think carefully about the reality of what you see on a movie screen. Remember, the devil makes the Capital Sin of Lust look much better than it really is. Don't become the victim of his manipulations. He did not earn the title Father of Lies because he is truthful.

Keep in mind that people who make movies are not interested in God's plan or the proper expression of sexual feelings. The making of movies is a business. The purpose of a business is to make money. Movie producers know that sexual urges are easily aroused and pleasurable. Hence, they focus on the entertaining or "fun" aspects of sexual expression. They fail to present you with the complications that so-called recreational sex can cause. Rather fantasy, humor, and pleasure are emphasized. Don't be tricked by the veneer of false promises.

4. Music

Music can be powerfully influential in forming our attitudes on the expression of sexual feelings. Music can help us to "chill out." It enables us to escape from the pressures of everyday living. For a moment, music can provide us with relief from our troubles. However, the messages that music conveys about the expression of sexual feelings can be dangerous. If you listen carefully to the lyrics, you will be able to recognize these. The melody, lyrics, and suggestive body movements of the singers can arouse lustful feelings, if you are not careful. The more you listen to such music, the more likely it is that you will become desensitized to these potentially-sinful influences.

The lyrics of some songs suggest that you give free reign to your sexual impulses. If two people are attracted to each other, this is called "love." The actual act of engaging in sexual activity is called "love-making." The use of the word "love" can cause you to become confused. Love is supposed to be a good thing. Love involves commitment, deep caring, and true respect for another human being. By using the word "love," the lyrics are putting lustful sexual expression and true love on the same level. This tricky use of words can lead you to believe that behaving immorally is "no big deal." Doesn't this sound like something that the Father of Lies would concoct in order to deceive you?

Make no mistake about it! The expression of sexual feelings outside of marriage is lust, not love. Commitment, care, and respect, which are the characteristics of true love between a man and a woman, are absent. Remember that experiencing physical pleasure is the goal of lust, not true love. Keep this distinction in mind. Confusing love with lust can make a big difference in how you view a relationship with another person. Think about these questions. How would God expect you to treat someone who you say you love? If you love another person, would you want to defile him or her by engaging in impure acts? Would you want to be defiled by someone, especially when this could lead to the damnation of your soul?

Again, when you listen to the lyrics of a song, be on guard. Are the words a true representation of love or are they misleading? Keep in mind that real love involves much more than songs convey. It is not simply physical attraction, pleasure, or sleeping with another person for one night.

5. Peers

Much of the information that you receive about sex may come from friends. For the most part, you are all exposed to the same advertisements, television programs, movies, and music. Some of your friends might become overly influenced by the media. They will become involved in early sexual relationships, failing to understand that the sin of Lust can be emotionally and spiritually destructive.

God made strict laws regarding the expression of sexual feelings. The failure to obey these laws will not go unpunished. Although you might think that there are no penalties for disobeying God, this is far from the truth. The devil wants you to focus on the pleasures associated with Lust. He can then lead you away from God and cloud your thinking. Once you are corrupted, you will be in the devil's pocket. You will become so spiritually deadened that your sinful behavior won't even bother you. And even if your conscience troubles you with guilt, you will lie to yourself and deny the truth. Isn't this what the Father of Lies intends? Wouldn't Satan use your friends to entrap you? Keep in mind that if your friends become the victims of Lust, they will try to justify their behavior. They will ignore God and argue that "having sex is no big deal" and "everybody does it." Some will insist that what they are doing is in-line with modern thinking. They will try to justify their sinful actions by claiming that, "we are living in the twenty-first century" and "waiting to have sex is old-fashioned." You have probably heard this before, and you will continue to hear it. What do you think about these justifications? When you enter the secular world, you will be subjected to this kind of thinking at all levels of society.

Remember, when people want to do something that is pleasurable but wrong, they will always make up reasons to justify their behavior. They will try to convince themselves that what they are doing is acceptable, even though they may be committing a mortal sin. In fact, they will try to convince you that you should follow their example. Would the devil want them to do otherwise?

Let's face it. There can be lots of short-term rewards for behaving as your friends do, even if what they are doing is sinful. Having sex can make you feel grownup. It can make you appear to be "cool." Sometimes young people engage in sexual activity because they want to fit in and be popular. Be careful of being influenced by peers who believe in these false promises. These so-called friends will give you the impression that they are mature and know more about life than they really do. If you allow yourself to be influenced by them, it will cost you your self-respect and seriously impair your relationship with God. However, the Father of Lies will be pleased with your rebellion. He will cheer you on. But like Adam and Eve, your rebellion will only leave you with feelings of shame, bitterness, and regret. Don't let so-called friends lead you to destruction.

One last point should be taken into account by you and your friends. Over the last decade, Satan, who is a technological wizard, has been bombarding you and young people like yourself with pornographic filth via the Internet. Printed and visual material such as books, photos, pictures, and videos of nude men and women engaging in erotic sexual activity are everywhere. The Internet has made pornography easily available to those who seek the pleasures that lustful self-indulgence promises.

Some of your friends might have entered these pornographic sites and tried to get you to do the same. Don't fall prey to this temptation! Keep in mind that pornography makes billions of dollars for those who promote and sell this moral filth. Those unfortunate victims, who purposely seek and dwell on this licentious material, risk becoming sex addicts. Remember, Lust is the number one weapon that Satan uses to lure young people like yourself into mortal sin. Satan "loves" pornography and hopes that you and your friends will "love" it too. Again, keep in mind, an addiction to pornography makes big-bucks for those who sell this moral poison. These disciples of the devil do not care about you or your friends. Once you are "hooked," feelings of guilt, shame, and remorse, instead of the sexual gratification you were promised, will soon follow. Don't be fooled. Playing with pornography is like playing with fire. It can burn you badly and lead to a serious addiction, which can ruin your life.

Lastly, as indicated previously, being in a Catholic environment, particularly over the last decade, has helped to protect you and your Catholic friends from the Father of Lies and his false promises. However, he has not given up in his attempts to capture your soul. Rather, he remains lurking in the shadows, waiting for the moment when you might be more vulnerable. Now is the time to plan ahead so that Satan isn't able to trick you into believing that defying God's Laws on human sexuality will lead you to an earthly paradise.

6. Society

Unfortunately, secular society is populated with many adults who think that trying to reason with adolescents is an impossible task. They believe that adolescents are incapable of controlling themselves. Many adults think most adolescents are "going to have sex anyway," no matter what they say. They adamantly contend that religious training, education, and stressing the importance of remaining chaste are unlikely to have any impact on your ability to think and exercise self-control. Do you agree with these adults?

Because many adults have little confidence in your ability to remain chaste, they emphasize the importance of protecting yourself from unwanted pregnancies, AIDS, and other diseases. Condoms and other birth control devices will be offered to you. They tell you that these will supposedly prevent you from suffering any negative consequences for your sinful behavior. In other words, you are being told that you can defy God's law and get away with it. This line of thinking, as noted previously, leaves you in a state of mortal sin. You already know the consequences of this. However, there are also psychological, emotional, and socially negative consequences attached to lustful behavior. These will be discussed later on in this Open Letter. You should note that these consequences manifest themselves immediately in this world. If you are not careful, the Father of Lies will not only capture your soul in the afterlife, but can make your life miserable here on earth as well.

The point to keep in mind, however, is that condoms, pills, and other birth control devices will not prevent you from facing the negative consequences of Lust. You will need a positive strategy in order to remain chaste. This can be achieved through prayer, receiving the sacraments, and living an active spiritual life. Don't let yourself become influenced by those who believe in Satan's false promises.

7. Fashions

Fashions primarily refer to the way we dress — the attire that we choose to clothe our bodies. To the thoughtless, this may sound like it's "no big deal." But this is a much bigger deal than we may think. Young people, like you, believe that they are quite capable of making good choices in this regard. However, whether they use a reasoned approach in making their selections is open to question. It appears that most young people simply observe what their role models and the so called "in-crowd" are wearing. They then select their clothes accordingly. Little or no thought goes into how they dress or the impact that this has on those around them.

The designers and manufacturers of clothing help to make the choosing of clothes a relatively easy task. They stock the stores with the latest attire. If you want different clothes, you have to go to a specialty store or order them from a catalogue. Tight jeans, skimpy bathing suits, hip-hugging pants, short pull-over shirts exposing one's midriff, and overly-revealing clothing are on the shelves and racks throughout the store.

This clothing, which is far from being modest, is designed for, marketed to, and purchased by both young and older females. The latter, who should know better, still aspire to be young and dress no differently than their daughters. Their on-going quest for youth rather than wisdom seems to dominate. This only erects a barrier between the older and younger generations. Because both generations have little or no understanding of the importance of modesty, they doom themselves to the problems that immodesty creates.

There is an old saying in the business world about products that sell easily and quickly: "These (products) are selling like hot cakes." We might say the same about impure attire: "Immodest clothing sells like hot cakes." Think about this for a few minutes. Interestingly, today's females are encouraged to dress in a way that is described as "looking hot." While some young women view "looking hot" as a compliment, this term really means that they easily arouse the sexual impulses of the men surrounding them. If you think about this, "looking hot" is hardly complimentary. It certainly is not the foundation for the development of a true loving relationship, which was discussed previously.

Again, notice that the latest fashions often focus on accentuating the shape of the female body. Hence, it is sex appeal rather than femininity that is emphasized in today's modern dress. Keep in mind that these fashions are designed to stimulate our passions, the sinful side of our human nature.

Femininity, which is considered to be archaic by today's standards, emphasizes the softer and gentler qualities of girls and women. For example, Julie Andrews in "The Sound of Music" optimized the notion of femininity in her dress and demeanor. This was one of the biggest money-making movies of all time and continues to be popular. However, today's "chic" modern females would ridicule Julie Andrews as being "old-fashioned" and "out of touch" with our current mode of dress and behavior.

Stop and think about this. Those women who choose to wear revealing clothing have turned themselves into sex objects. Men might smile as they pass by; they may compliment them on how they look; and they might pay lots of attention to those females who wear "hot" clothing. But it is not affection that draws this special attention. Rather, quick sexual arousal and thoughts of passionate pleasure with this woman are the driving force behind this attentiveness.

If you are a young lady, you should ask yourself these questions: Is this the kind of attention that I really want from a young man? Do I want to be thought of as a sex object, whose only purpose is to provide selfish pleasure to a person who is just pretending to be interested in me? Or do I want to be thought of as someone who is not only physically attractive but has desirable personal qualities as well? Answer these questions honestly. Don't let Lust cloud your judgment.

Keep in mind that the way you dress sends a message to those who observe you. If you say that the way you dress is not intended to be immodest, but you wear overly tight and revealing clothing, the message that you convey will be the opposite of this. Consider the following quote by Saint Jerome: "Either we must speak as we dress, or dress what we speak. Why do we profess one thing and display another? The tongue talks of chastity, but the whole body reveals impurity."

Saint Jerome's quote says it all. If you are a young woman, you must decide how you want to be viewed by the young men in your life. The way you dress and conduct yourself will have a profound impact on what they really think about you. Don't allow yourself to be influenced by those who confuse Lust with love. Which of these would you prefer — being truly loved or an object of another person's Lust? The choice is yours.

Although females may be responsible for the arousal of a male's sexual passion, the man's thoughts and behavior following what he sees are major contributors to the sin of Lust. It is true that men become more quickly aroused than females. However, this does not give them an excuse to fall prey to the devil's temptations. Rather, fending off these temptations, although this is difficult, will be necessary. Saying a "Hail Mary" to Our Blessed Mother will help you. Moreover, during these times it will be important to keep the following questions and answers in the forefront of your mind: Is this the kind of girl who I want to date and to meet my parents? How about my friends? Do they view her as being "hot"? What would they think if I told them I was dating her? How would Our Lord and His mother view my decision?

Believe it or not, most young men want chaste girlfriends. These virginal young ladies arouse gentle, protective, and chivalrous feelings within them. They don't want girlfriends who are promiscuous. Boys who date virtuous young ladies are proud to be seen with them. Dating a cheap girl is another matter. You will find that your friends will snidely smile or make an indecent comment when her name is mentioned. Even if they say nothing, just knowing what they are thinking can be embarrassing.

Finally, even though immodest clothing is all around you, take heart in knowing that Our Blessed Mother supports you in your fight to remain chaste. In fact, Our Lady of Fatima in the year 1917 said, "Certain fashions will be introduced that will offend Our Lord very much." This revelation occurred over ninety years ago when fashions were far from what they are today!

The fashions that Our Lady referred to as being "introduced" have finally arrived in clothing stores throughout the world. Satan's temptations are now in full force. It is up to you, young Catholic men and women, to maintain your ideals in the torrid sexual climate surrounding you. In order to combat this, keep an image of Our Blessed Mother, the model of purity, in the forefront of your mind. The imprinting of this image will help you to "crush the head of the serpent," whose sole purpose is to lead you to damnation.

8. Adult Role Models

Unfortunately, some of the adults whom you may admire behave sinfully. On the one hand they might tell you to avoid premarital sex. On the other hand, however, they might act as though sex was a playful activity.

For example, some boys receive mixed messages from those men who they admire. While they might not openly encourage boys to engage in premarital sex, they might not discourage it either. Some men view sexual activity with consenting females as a conquest or a verification of their masculinity. They might openly boast about this to their friends. When a female responds to their advances, some men believe that this occurs because they are so physically attractive that females cannot resist them. This, of course, is then viewed by these men as a verification of their manliness. Notice how self-centered and arrogant this manner of thinking happens to be. If you are a young woman, would you want to be involved with a man who thinks in this way? Like the Father of Lies, some men can be charming and tell you what they think you want to hear. Believe it or not, like Eve, you can be tricked by these deceptions if you are not careful.

Keep in mind that some young men will try to flatter you in their attempts to lead you astray.

They might even say they love you so that you will consent to their advances. However, behind your back your promiscuity will be a topic of conversation with their friends and you will be labeled as being "easy." Boys, on the other hand, are often excused for behaving sinfully. They might be thought of as being manly if they have had multiple sexual encounters. Grown men, who should know better, will sometimes excuse their promiscuous behavior. They will claim that "boys will be boys" and "men need sex more than women." Ask yourself: Would God agree with this kind of thinking?

If you are a young man, you might know some adults who believe in the above. You could easily fall into the trap of thinking that premarital sex is "no big deal."

Why is this so? you might ask. The answer to this question is simple enough. You will be told that sexual expression is natural. And if you are a man, it is "too difficult to expect you to control yourself." Do you believe this? How would Our Lord respond to this question?

Girls, as well as boys, receive mixed messages from adults. You have probably noticed that some very attractive adult females dress and act in a way which encourages sexual advances. Their clothing might be very tight and revealing, flaunting their body parts. Obviously, they dress this way in order to draw attention to themselves, even though they might deny this. Remember Saint Jerome? While these adult women are not openly saying that they approve of lustful sex, their behavior and dress indicate otherwise. In fact, their attire and actions encourage lustful thinking and promiscuity.

Finally, you will see adult males and females who have affairs with many different partners. Some adults will openly admit that this is the way they choose to live. Moreover, they will insist there is nothing wrong with this behavior, arguing that they aren't hurting anyone. Because they are consenting adults, they believe that they can do as they please. Certainly these adults have the choice to behave lustfully. God has given them free will. However, do they have the right to live in this way? Keep in mind that God has never given us the *right* to break His laws. He has only given us the *choice* to do so.

Remember, some adults will tell you that promiscuity is wrong while setting a bad example themselves. Adults, like children and adolescents, commit sins. They are not perfect. While you might look up to adults, you must decide to do what is right. When you see adults behaving badly, you must try not to be influenced by this. It's up to you to seek God's help and control your thoughts and actions.

9. Consequences of Lust

It's time to pull together the contents of this Open Letter by focusing on the potentially devastating consequences of the Capital Sin of Lust and how this can ruin your life. Remember to be on the alert! You will be entering a world filled with people who will try to convince you that there are no negative consequences for unchaste behavior. If you have friends who behave immorally, they will try to justify their sinful actions and encourage you to follow their example. You will find that these so-called friends have an unrealistic view of the consequences of behaving unchastely. Moreover, they will have a false sense of invincibility, which leads them into believing that nothing bad will happen to them, even though they are violating God's laws. This is dangerous thinking that will get them into serious trouble.

Keep in mind that listening to unchaste companions can spike your curiosity. Your attention to their impure talk, jokes, and exploits not only places you in an occasion of sin, but can heighten your desire to act like them. Like Eve, whose curiosity led to mortal sin, you too can fall prey to Satan's temptations.

As noted previously, peer pressure to behave unchastely can be great. The desire to be accepted and popular and to be viewed as mature and independent can cloud your judgment. Avoiding the notion that you are "old-fashioned," and trying to appear "cool" instead, can lead you into being influenced by immoral friends. Don't let such shallow reasoning cause you to act impurely. If you are seeking love, behaving impurely will not bring this about. Rather, degradation and the loss of your integrity will be your reward. This will not approve of lustful sex, their behavior and dress indicate otherwise. In fact, their attire and actions encourage lustful thinking and promiscuity.

Finally, you will see adult males and females who have affairs with many different partners. Some adults will openly admit that this is the way they choose to live. Moreover, they will insist there is nothing wrong with this behavior, arguing that they aren't hurting anyone. Because they are consenting adults, they believe that they can do as they please. Certainly these adults have the choice to behave lustfully. God has given them free will. However, do they have the right to live in this way? Keep in mind that God has never given us the *right* to break His laws. He has only given us the *choice* to do so.

Remember, some adults will tell you that promiscuity is wrong while setting a bad example themselves. Adults, like children and adolescents, commit sins. They are not perfect. While you might look up to adults, you must decide to do what is right. When you see adults behaving badly, you must try not to be influenced by this. It's up to you to seek God's help and control your thoughts and actions.

9. Consequences of Lust

It's time to pull together the contents of this Open Letter by focusing on the potentially devastating consequences of the Capital Sin of Lust and how this can ruin your life. Remember to be on the alert! You will be entering a world filled with people who will try to convince you that there are no negative consequences for unchaste behavior. If you have friends who behave immorally, they will try to justify their sinful actions and encourage you to follow their example. You will find that these so-called friends have an unrealistic view of the consequences of behaving unchastely. Moreover, they will have a false sense of invincibility, which leads them into believing that nothing bad will happen to them, even though they are violating God's laws. This is dangerous thinking that will get them into serious trouble.

Keep in mind that listening to unchaste companions can spike your curiosity. Your attention to their impure talk, jokes, and exploits not only places you in an occasion of sin, but can heighten your desire to act like them. Like Eve, whose curiosity led to mortal sin, you too can fall prey to Satan's temptations.

As noted previously, peer pressure to behave unchastely can be great. The desire to be accepted and popular and to be viewed as mature and independent can cloud your judgment. Avoiding the notion that you are "old-fashioned," and trying to appear "cool" instead, can lead you into being influenced by immoral friends. Don't let such shallow reasoning cause you to act impurely. If you are seeking love, behaving impurely will not bring this about. Rather, degradation and the loss of your integrity will be your reward. This will not enable you to acquire the maturity, independence, or popularity which you seek.

It is important to keep in mind that the negative consequences of defying God's law occur in this world as well as the next. This is referred to as the "temporal punishment of sin." In other words, those who are unchaste will be forced to deal with a number of unpleasant practical problems right here on earth. First and foremost is the loss of grace resulting in mortal sin. This will condemn your soul to Hell for all eternity. Is this worth a few moments of sensual pleasure? Some of the other practical problems that you might face are as follows:

(a) Loss of your virginity. This is a treasure that once lost can never be regained. You can seek God's forgiveness and receive the Sacrament of Penance after the sinful act. This will restore your relationship with God and make amends for offending Him. However, the loss of your virginity can never be undone. Think about this before it happens. Is it worth it?

(b) Loss of your reputation. Your reputation will be ruined. Although you may not be confronted openly, those who have maintained their integrity will think of you as a person with loose moral standards. Behind your back, you will be called a "slut" or some other derogatory label. Is this the way you want to be referred to by others?

(c) Contraction of a disease. Don't minimize the possibility of contracting a disease. Imagine the embarrassment of having to be treated by your family physician if this occurred. Perhaps you would try to hide this from your parents and seek treatment from a clinic without their authorization. How would this affect your relationship with your parents and other members of your family? How would you feel if you had to face this problem? What about the consequences of contracting a disease in which the symptoms might be treatable but the disease itself cannot be cured? In other words, you would have to live permanently with the disease and periodically treat the symptoms as they appear. (Herpes, for example.) Consider this before it happens and keep in mind that this could happen to you.

(d) Abusive relationships. Unchaste behavior can lead to you being abused by your partner. Arguing, cursing, and violence toward one another occur when young people are corrupted by Lust. They soon lose respect for each other and their behavior becomes vulgar and crude. Is this the kind of relationship that you would want? This would be the reward for losing your innocence.

(e) Single parenthood. Single parenthood means that you will be totally responsible for your child should you become pregnant. There will be no engagement ring, wedding, honeymoon, or spouse to help you. Your child will eventually learn that he or she was born out of Lust, not love—an accident that resulted when you and your partner were seeking pleasure. How would you feel if you were this child? What would the child think about being conceived out of wedlock? How would you explain this to your child? If you are a female, there is another problem that you will face should you became pregnant out of wedlock. There are those who will tell you to get an abortion. The devil will make this option particularly attractive. He will promise that all of your troubles will cease if you take advantage of this simple medical procedure. He will emphasize that abortions are safe and legal—besides, "everybody does it." What do you think about this line of reasoning? What would you do if you became pregnant? How would your partner act if this happened? What would God expect you to do?

(f) The loss of self-respect resulting in substance abuse. Lust can quickly lead to self-hatred and the loss of self-respect. In order to dull the emotional pain, the use of drugs and alcohol, which are referred to as "self-medication," soon follow. These can not only lead to addiction, but might be the cause of an accidental death or suicide. How would you feel if you took an overdose of pills and had to face Our Lord for your final judgment?

As you can see, the "temporal punishment of sin" occurs right here on earth, in the here and now. Lust could not only cause you to lose your soul, but you will suffer in this present life. God will not be mocked. Keep this in mind before you violate His commandments.

"O Mary, conceived without sin, pray for us who have recourse to thee." Our Blessed Mother, our model of purity and chastity, may she protect and strengthen you, "the salt of the earth" and "the light of the world" as you enter a secular society that is obsessed with Lust and its false promises.

III

Open letter on how psychology can help you

On using Catholic psychology to combat capital sins

FROM: PAUL LAVIN, PH.D.

Dear Graduate,

Throughout this book, the ways in which the devil uses the Capital Sins to capture the souls of unsuspecting and naïve Catholics has been stressed. This Open Letter will focus on psychological strategies that you, "the salt of the earth," can put into practice to help you in this battle. As emphasized previously, moral and spiritual rot is so prevalent that we have become blinded to this mounting corruption.

We might compare ourselves to the proverbial frog in a pot of cold water. The pot is placed on a hot stove. The poor creature fails to recognize that he is about to be boiled alive. Because the progression leading to this bad end is gradual, the unsuspecting frog basks in the water, adjusting to the slowly rising temperature. Once the water hits the boiling point, it is too late. The frog might sense that his life is in jeopardy, but not in time to jump out of the pot. So he is unable to save himself.

Those who fail to recognize the seriousness of the Capital Sins are likely to suffer a worse fate than the unsuspecting frog. Unlike the frog, we have an immortal soul. If left unprotected, our soul can become corrupted by the devil and condemned to the fires of Hell for eternity. Spiritually-lackadaisical men and women are grist for the devil's mill. Remember, his sinful temptations will appear to be harmless and attractive. In order to lure you into sin, the devil will fill your mind with carefully-crafted words and phrases. He will then create thoughts and images promising much. When acted upon, however, these will be far from meeting your expectations.

As a clinical psychologist, I have come to appreciate the importance of words and how these influence our emotions and the choices that we make. What we say to ourselves—the actual words, phrases, and sentences—have a major impact on how we feel and act. The devil, who is an expert on our fallen nature, crafts his language accordingly. The Father of Lies knows our weaknesses. He uses words to exploit our vulnerabilities and lure us into doing his bidding. As noted previously, Adam and Eve are a good example of this.

Good and evil are at war with each other. The first step in combating the Capital Sins is to identify these forces and to describe the ongoing battle between them. For example, as children we were taught that two spiritual beings inhabited each of our shoulders—the devil was on the left and our Guardian Angel was on the right. Each had access to one of our corresponding ears. The devil was forever whispering into our left ear, encouraging us to follow the ways of the world. Our Guardian

Angel, on the other hand, whispered into our right ear, stressing the importance of following God's laws. These battles involved verbal fist-fights, actual debates between these warring spirits, one promoting evil and the other advocating good. It was up to us to distinguish between the truth and lies and to choose wisely. The presence of our Guardian Angel and his guidance were taken seriously. We were encouraged to listen carefully to his counsel, believing that the failure to do so could cost us the salvation of our soul.

Being more aware of the interior warfare between good and evil and acquiring the ability to monitor and control its outcome is important to your salvation. In order to achieve this goal, two tasks must be mastered: (1) First, we must learn to identify those thoughts which fan the fires of temptation and make it appear so attractive; and (2) we need to formulate counter-thoughts to replace these so that we don't fall prey to the devil's lure. These counter-thoughts will consist of Catholic language, actual words and sentences, based on our Faith and how it should be put into practice.

Understanding and Controlling Spiritual Warfare

The following is an example on how this model works:

Let's pretend that you and your friend are students at the same university. Your friend is very intelligent. He hardly ever studies, but continually gets excellent grades. You, on the other hand, have to work extra hard in order to do well. An important exam is scheduled at the end of the term. You study every day in preparation for the exam. Your friend, however, does little studying. On the day before the exam, he crams for a few hours and then watches television for the rest of the evening. You study right into the night, foregoing the pleasure of watching your favorite TV shows. The next day you both take the exam. Your friend gets a grade of 95. You get a grade of 85, which is ten points less. Your friend gloats over his superior performance. He even boasts about how well he did with so little effort.

At first you feel disappointed. You really think that you deserved a better grade. It is at this point that the devil begins to work on you. He tells you that you were "cheated" and how unfair this is in light of your effort. The more you think about this, the more resentful you become. As you continue to ruminate, you become furious and even jealous because the work is so easy for your friend. The following thoughts keep running through your mind: "These test results are grossly unfair. I worked much harder than him. It's not right that he should do better than me. He's got the nerve to brag about how smart he is and how little he studied. What a sap I am! Hard work doesn't count for anything. What a rip off! I wish that he would fall on his face and get what's coming to him. I hate him and everything that he stands for!"

Notice how this situation began with feelings of disappointment because you were hoping to get an A on the exam. This sounds reasonable. After all, you spent much of your time studying and you wanted to get the highest grade possible for your effort. However, note how a change occurred when the devil plied your mind with thoughts of self-pity and resentment. Your disappointment escalated into fury because you believed you were "ripped off" — cheated from receiving the grade you thought you rightly deserved. Moreover, you then started to become envious of your friend's ability. This accelerated into hate and the desire for revenge: "I wish he would fall on his face and get what's coming to him." What you are saying to yourself is that you wish that your friend would come to a bad end. Becoming furious, vengeful, and envious violates God's law. As you can see, unless this dangerous thinking is stopped and corrected, it could lead to mortal sin and put the salvation of your soul in jeopardy.

Let's suppose, however, that you recognized that your thinking was becoming destructive and you decided to put a stop to it. You then consciously attempted to replace your self-destructive thinking with the following counter-thoughts:

> "I am disappointed that I did not get an A on the examination. However, I gave it my best effort and I did get a solid B. It's true that my friend, who studied far less than me, received an A. I could continue to think that

this is unfair, believing that I was cheated because I worked harder than him. However, this will cause me to become bitter, vengeful, and envious. Better that I accept my friend's success as God's will. Otherwise, I will become angry with God, furious with my friend, and jealous because his academic ability is superior to my own. This is a sin of Pride. In fact, my friend's boasting occurred because of this. Rather than being thankful to God for his superior intellect, he takes full credit for his success. It's a pity that he does not see this and change what he is doing."

Imagine how you would feel if you were able to curb your self-destructive thoughts and replace these with the latter. The spiritual warfare within you would cease and you would experience inner peace. Instead of resentment, rage, and envy, you would be content with yourself and thankful for what you achieved. Moreover, you would feel compassion for your friend, who is drowning in a sea of Pride, the most deadly of all the Capital Sins. Your change in thinking might even motivate you to confront your friend and encourage him to make better use of the talent that God has given him. This would be an act of charity and it is charity that makes you a good friend. Isn't this what Our Lord would expect and wouldn't such an act bring you closer to Him? And how might your friend respond to your act of kindness? Although there is no guarantee, it might increase your respect in his eyes, and teach him what true friendship and loyalty mean.

As you can see, the preceding scenario is an example of how Catholic thinking can be used to combat thoughts leading to the corruption of your soul. Catholic thinking consists of the actual words, phrases, sentences, and questions that you might say to yourself when temptations such as envy, vengeance, and pride should arise. It should be kept in mind that all temptations come from the devil. Again, recall how Satan tempted Eve. Eve did not ask the devil to tempt her. Rather, he slyly planted thoughts of disobedience in her mind. The more Eve thought about disobeying God, the greater the temptation became. Her thoughts about eating the forbidden fruit and being like God intensified. Eve failed to stop and counter her sinful thoughts. As a result, Pride got the best of her and she did the devil's bidding.

An important point to keep in mind is that there are few of us who openly ask for the devil to tempt us. Rather, like a thief in the night, he sneaks up on us, invading our minds with temptations, which appeal to our fallen human nature. Because our human nature is flawed and sin is so appealing, we often fail to see its danger. Instead of nipping these temptations in the bud, like Eve, we can dwell upon and nurture sinful thoughts until we are overcome by them. This is why Catholic thinking is so important. It can stop and replace sinful thoughts before they impair our relationship with God and destroy us.

Needless to say, learning to use Catholic language in order to combat sinful thinking, which comes from the Father of Lies, is not easy. It requires that we master our intellect and will, our higher faculties. Mastering these is far less attractive than the temptations offered by Satan. This is what makes the task so difficult. Learning to use Catholic language demands that we examine our conscience. We must make an honest appraisal of what we are truly thinking and make a persistent effort to put what we learn into practice. Above all, we must have a sincere desire to follow God's plan. Catholic language is actually a form of prayer. It can help us to cooperate with God's graces, which He provides at our times of trial. Using Catholic language can be a valuable weapon for combating the devil, whose purpose is to capture your soul.

Applying Catholic Language to the Capital Sins

As noted previously, the Capital Sins are as follows: (1) Pride; (2) Greed; (3) Lust; (4) Anger; (5) Gluttony; (6) Envy; and (7) Sloth. In the next section, each Capital Sin and the language that the Father of Lies might use to tempt us is presented. The language consists of actual words, phrases, and sentences, which are designed to appeal to our lower nature and encourage Sinful Thinking (ST). Following each Capital Sin and its accompanying ST, Catholic Language (CL) provides the actual words, phrases, and sentences that you can use to stop ST once it is presented. Notice that CL not only involves the use of Catholic principles but includes references to Holy Scripture, which can be helpful in forming your thoughts as well.

In putting the above into practice, the following steps need to be taken. First, as soon as you experience the temptation to sin, ask yourself this question: "What am I saying to myself that is leading me into temptation?" Second, try to write down the actual words occurring in your mind at that moment. Recording your thoughts will not only improve your self-knowledge, but it will help you to check and stop ST before the temptation worsens and you become overwhelmed. Once the ST is identified, the third step requires that you try to formulate CL, which can be used to combat and replace ST. The actual writing of CL would be best when you are first learning how to apply this approach. With repeated practice, you will become more skilled and form better thinking habits in coping with the devil and his false promises.

It should be kept in mind that writing down your thoughts can be annoying, particularly when Satan is tempting you. In fact, avoiding the writing of your thoughts will be a temptation. Satan would much prefer that you "chill out" and "go with the flow," especially when this is leading you astray. He will appeal to the slothful side of your human nature, planting thoughts in your mind such as: "Having to go to this extreme — writing down your thoughts — is silly and a waste of your time and effort." There are a number of excuses that he will help you to concoct in order to weaken your resolve.

Writing your thoughts in a journal will require that you train your intellect and control your will. This leads to the acquisition of self-discipline. Self-discipline is hated by the devil who wants you to become a prisoner of your senses. Like any difficult task, writing your thoughts and learning to control them will become easier with continued practice. Eventually, the writing and extra deliberation will not be necessary. You will be able to "automatically" put this into practice as the need arises. However, this goal can only be achieved with hard work and persistence. And remember, the devil has no intention of making this easy for you.

Using CL to Combat ST

Each Capital Sin and the ST accompanying it will be presented in this section. Keep in mind that if ST is not stopped, it will not only intensify the temptation, but could lead to the violation of God's laws. Following each ST, the CL which can be used to replace that ST will be offered. Again, the CL is based on Catholic principles and Holy Scripture.

PRIDE (ST): "Because I am talented, intelligent, and have money, I am better than other people. My superiority entitles me to special treatment. Being wealthy places me in a higher social class and that's what counts. People who are poor and lack social class are below me and should be viewed with contempt and treated accordingly."

PRIDE (CL): "We are all equal in the eyes of God. Those who are given talents will be expected to develop them and use these to serve Him. They will be held accountable if they fail to do so. God will be pleased if I use my gifts for the betterment of mankind. However, He will be displeased if I boast or use my gifts to laud my superiority over others. Remember the Parable of the Talents (Matthew 25:14-30). God was equally pleased with the servant who had five talents and doubled these as with the servant who had two talents and did the same. God is concerned with my spiritual welfare. He will not judge me according to my social status, wealth, or popularity. God abhors arrogance and prizes humility. Throughout His earthly life, Jesus demonstrated for us perfect charity and humility. This is the standard upon which He will judge me."

GREED (ST): "More is always better than less. The man who has acquired the most money and possessions is the winner in the quest for a good life. I can never have enough money or possessions. The more that I own, the better protected I will be against any misfortune that might arise."

GREED (CL): "God does not care about wealth and material possessions. He repeatedly warned us that the accumulation of money and worldly goods could seriously hinder us in the pursuit of Heaven. In fact, Christ instructed the Apostles to do the following: 'Sell what you have and give alms. Make for yourself purses that do not grow old, a treasure unfailing in Heaven, where neither thief draws nor moth destroys. For where your treasure is, there will your heart be' (Luke 12:33-34). Think of all the times that Christ instructed others to give up their worldly wealth and said, 'Come follow me.' If Christ expected the Apostles to heed His teachings, it makes sense that He would expect this from me as well."

LUST (ST): "The desire to have sex is perfectly natural. God intended this or He wouldn't have put these feelings within me. I have the right to have sex as long as I'm not hurting anybody. It's my body and I should be able to do with it as I please."

LUST (CL): "The primary purpose for God's creation of sexual feelings is to ensure the procreation of the human race. God intended for these to be pleasurable. However, He expects that the expression of these should occur between a married man and woman. Outside of the union between husband and wife, sexual behavior is mortally sinful and could lead to the loss of my soul. Moreover, behaving promiscuously will lead me to lose my virginity and tarnish my reputation. My virginity, once lost, can never be restored. My reputation may be regained with much effort, but this behavior will forever be a stain on my past."

ANGER (ST): "The world should be fair. If I get cheated, I should be able to get even. An eye for an eye and a tooth for a tooth is only fair. The authorities should provide justice to make sure that this happens. If they fail to do so, I have the right to take matters into my own hands. Vengeance belongs to me."

ANGER (CL): "The world has never been a fair place. This is why God has promised us that we will be judged by Him. Each of us will be held accountable for each *iota* of His law. He, not the world, will give us perfect justice. God commanded us to treat our enemies with charity."

As I mentioned in a previous letter, Saint Paul (Romans 12:19-21) wrote: "Do not avenge yourselves, beloved, for it is written, Vengeance is Mine; I will repay says the Lord. But if your enemy is hungry, give him food; if he is thirsty, give him drink; for by doing, you will heap hot coals upon his head. Be not overcome with evil but overcome evil with good. I must leave justice to God and trust that He will fulfill His promise. If I treat my enemy charitably, I will be 'heaping hot coals of fire upon his head.' What better form of justice could there be?"

GLUTTONY (ST): "Super-size is better than smaller-size. Better to have too much food and drink than too little. There is nothing like an all-you-can-eat buffet. Naturally I'm going to eat as much as I can because I'm paying for it. Thanksgiving is a special holiday when you are expected to eat until you get stuffed. That's what it's all about. You know the old saying, 'Eat, drink, and be merry, for tomorrow we die.'"

GLUTTONY (CL): "Eating and drinking to excess is self-indulgent and weakens my ability to control myself. The importance of being temperate in my eating and drinking habits is stressed throughout the Church's teachings and Holy Scripture. Christ fasted for forty days in the desert before being tempted by the devil. John the Baptist and all the great saints ate and drank temperately. Temperance is a virtue that strengthens my will and prevents me from debasing my body and soul. Gluttony will turn me into an obese and degenerate human being."

ENVY (ST): "Look at the good things that happen to him and he doesn't work hard or worship as fervently as I do. His parents let him do what he pleases and give him everything he wants. I have to work for everything that I get and my parents watch me like a hawk. To top it off, he's popular, smart, and good at sports. I wish I had his talents. He gets away with stuff I would never get away with."

ENVY (CL): "My friend is fortunate that he is so talented. However, the way that he acts is not pleasing to God. His parents, by giving him everything that he wants and failing to supervise him, are neglecting their responsibility. This could lead to trouble in the future. My parents, on the other hand, are diligent and protective because they want me to be prepared to face life's challenges in the years to come. Dwelling on my friend's good fortune is only making me resentful and envious. Christ commanded that I love my neighbor as myself. However, being envious only prevents me from fulfilling this responsibility. Christ warned us not to be envious of evildoers and those who have more worldly goods than us. Rather, we should behave charitably toward them. Being uncharitable will only worsen my envy and destroy me."

SLOTH (ST): "If something is not interesting, fun, or easy, I shouldn't have to do it. It's the teacher's fault for not motivating me to do the work. Boring tasks should be avoided. Saying prayers is boring too. In the rosary, you say the same prayers over and over again. No wonder I get distracted and don't say it as often as I should. It's not my fault. Doing things should not be so difficult. If I skip my prayers, God will understand."

SLOTH (CL): "Sloth is unacceptable to God. He commands that we make good use of our talents and will punish those who fail to do so. The Parable of the Gold Pieces is a good example of this (Luke 19:12-26). The nobleman in this parable gave ten servants ten pieces of gold and instructed them to trade with these until he returned. Two of the servants made a profit as a result of their trading. The third servant, however, wrapped the gold piece in a napkin, saving it until the master returned. It was toward this servant that the master directed his wrath. He was referred to as the 'wicked servant' for failing to make any effort to increase what was given to him. The servant was not only admonished, but the gold piece was taken from him. He was left with nothing. I can't let laziness cause me to become a wicked servant. I have an obligation to God to develop those talents that He has given me. I would rather be praised by God then incur His wrath."

It should be noted that CL can be applied to all of the various sins leading to spiritual destruction. For example, the sin of Presumption (a sin against the Holy Ghost) is quite prevalent today. The ST attached to the sin of Presumption would be as follows: "God is too merciful to send anyone to Hell. If Hell exists at all, nobody would be in it. God loves us too much to let this happen. Besides, I'm a 'good person.' How could I ever be condemned to Hell?"

To counter the preceding, the following CL is offered: "It is true that God is all-merciful, but He is all-just as well. God promised that each *iota* of His law must be fulfilled and that we would be held accountable for even the smallest infraction. Christ emphatically said that Hell exists and those who failed to keep His commandments would be sent there."

And what about the sins that cry out to Heaven for vengeance, the sin of Sodomy, for example? The ST attached to this is as follows: "God made me this way (homosexual or lesbian). I have no control over this predisposition. It's in the genes. Certainly God understands this because He created me. I have the right to engage in sexual activity with my 'significant other' and live my 'alternate lifestyle' as I choose. Anyone who disagrees with me is a bigot or is homophobic."

The CL to counter this is as follows: "Throughout Holy Scripture, God condemned the Sin of Sodomy. God did not put two males or two females into the Garden of Eden. He created a man and woman as the natural parents of the human race. 'Whereas a man shall leave father and mother, and cleave to his wife; and they shall become one flesh' (Genesis 2:24). The marriage bond of 'one man, one woman, until death do they part,' is so essential that by the inspiration of the Holy Ghost this injunction is repeated three times in the New Testament (Matthew 5:32; Mark 10:2-12; Ephesians 5: 21-33)."

Summary and Conclusions

The importance of words and their meaning can have a powerful influence on your emotions, the choices that you make, and how you act. The Father of Lies has concocted his own lexicon of carefully-crafted words, phrases, and sentences which are designed to encourage you to engage in worldly pursuits that are contrary to God's will. The devil, who is an expert in exploiting our individual weaknesses, uses language to lull us into a spiritual stupor. Once this is achieved, he fills our minds with sinful thoughts and images which promise much, but fall far short of our expectations.

In order to combat the devil's plan, we need to identify those sinful thoughts and put a stop to them before they overwhelm us. Catholic

Language, which is based on Catholic principles and Holy Scripture, is used to replace these. Because the Father of Lies crafts language and images appealing to our lower nature, mastering our intellect and will so that this approach can be applied demands much effort. The devil will tempt you to avoid this task, telling you to "lighten up" and "not to take life so seriously." Don't fall prey to this clever manipulation. It is clear, concise, and straight-forward Catholic thinking that is needed to combat Satan's stranglehold on those spiritually-dulled persons who are unwittingly following him into damnation.

Saint Michael, the Archangel, protect our young Catholic men and women, "the salt of the earth" and "the light of the world," from the wiles and snares of the crafty Father of Lies.

IV

Open letter on preparing for the end of life

On the final judgment

FROM: PAUL LAVIN, PH.D.

Dear Graduate,

Throughout this book, we have focused on the Capital Sins and how the devil will exaggerate their attractiveness in order to lure you away from your Catholic Faith. The devil's goal is to get you to join his army — an army composed of Disciples of the World. They not only lead sinful lives, but try to influence others to do the same. If you believe that committing sin is "no big deal," you will be making the devil's job an easy one. As stressed in the Open Letters, your spiritual defenses may become so weakened that you will simply fall from one temptation to the next. Like most human beings who consider themselves to be "good persons," you will fail to see how spiritually lax you have become and how offensive your sinful actions are to God. Pray to Our Blessed Mother that you do not die in such a self-deceptive state.

In light of the preceding, I offer this last Open Letter on the purpose of life. This final letter focuses on our death and that which follows immediately thereafter. Keep this in mind: No matter how much wealth you accumulate, how famous you become, or how many earthly friends you have made, death puts a final end to all of these. Memories of days gone by, awards that you have won, and the class reunions you once attended will be mere shadows of the past. These will account for little or nothing when you stand before God and receive His final judgment. Rather, God's evaluation and how you used the time accorded to you will be all that matters. For any person who takes his or her Catholic Faith seriously, this must be a most frightening thought. Think about it. Eternal happiness or eternal damnation hang in the balance. There will be no reprieve or second chance. You will receive one or the other. How you have lived in God's eyes, not those of your friends, relatives, or business associates, is what will count.

The Open Letters have repeatedly focused upon the challenges that you will encounter in trying to keep your Catholic Faith when you enter secular society. Hopefully this material will be convincing enough to help you to stay on the right path. However, thinking about our final judgment can clearly drive home the seriousness of remaining faithful to Jesus Christ and His Church.

Again, thinking about the final judgment can be frightening. However, it must be reflected upon to ensure that we do not become victims of our own spiritual laxity. Because Jesus is gentle, kind, and merciful, we are quick to overlook that He is also all-just and will hold us accountable for the least violation of His law. Jesus warned that we should fear Him because He, and only He, has the power to condemn both our body and soul.

For instance, in the Gospel of Saint Luke (12:1-5), Christ said to His disciples:

> "Beware of the leaven of the Pharisees, which is hypocrisy. But there is nothing concealed that will not be disclosed, and nothing hidden that will not be made known. For what you have said in the darkness will be said in the light, and what you have whispered in the inner chambers will be preached on the housetops. But I say to you my friends, do not be afraid of those who kill the body, and after that have nothing more that they can do. But I will show you whom to be afraid of; be afraid of him who, after he has killed, has the power to cast into Hell. Yes, I say to you be afraid of him."

This clearly indicates that Christ expects us to have a healthy fear of Him and His power to reward or punish us. It is true that Jesus was gentle and meek, but He was not the "soft touch" that presumptuous persons make Him out to be. His words forthrightly indicate this. Be assured that Christ meant what He said. His final judgment of our soul will be a serious matter. Keep this in mind when secular-minded people try to influence you to give up your Faith in Christ and His Church.

In order to prepare you to think more deeply on the seriousness of the final judgment, consider the following. You will be on your own when the final judgment takes place. You will not have a team of clever lawyers, family members, or close friends who will be allowed to plead for the salvation of your soul. The blatant truth of how you lived your life will be fully disclosed to all interested parties involved in your case. And who are the interested parties? Our Lord Jesus Christ, Who will make the final judgment; your Guardian Angel, who was supposed to protect and provide for your spiritual welfare; and the devil, who wants your soul condemned to the fires of Hell. These are the principal parties involved in your case. Imagine yourself appearing before this tribunal. Imagine waiting to be judged. What might you be thinking and feeling about that which is to come?

Think about what is to follow. Perhaps your Guardian Angel will make the first attempt to plead your case. However, during the course of his presentation, he might begin to falter, recalling the times that you failed to follow his advice or accept God's grace when it was offered to you. He might valiantly try to emphasize your meritorious actions, but will these be enough to offset your many violations of God's law? There might be a slight quivering and nervousness in his demeanor as he completes his presentation.

Now imagine the devil. He is lurking in the shadows, fervently waiting to make the case that your soul belongs to him. He cites past blasphemies, sacrilegious Holy Communions, moments of debauchery and intoxication, and sins of the flesh. He forcefully points to the times when you carelessly disregarded the teachings of Christ's Church. And what about the jokes and mockery that you participated in even though you claimed to be a practicing Catholic?

Who will win the battle for your soul? Will your Guardian Angel prevail? Or will the devil be victorious because of the damning evidence that you so carelessly provided for him? Imagine that all of this is taking place right now. Imagine the intense anxiety that you would be experiencing. Imagine the final verdict to be delivered by Our Lord Himself. The time to think about this is now, before you enter secular society—before you are tempted by the many distractions which can lead you astray.

To think about the preceding is not particularly uplifting. At this point you might say to yourself, "I am young and it is natural for me to want to live a care-free life and participate in all that it has to offer." Who, in their youthful years, wants to reflect on the Last Judgment, especially when we think that there are so many more years before this will occur? But reflect on this you must. The salvation of your soul may depend on it. The longevity of one's life cannot be taken for granted. We can never be sure when God will call us and hold us accountable for our time on earth. Death is not something that only happens to old people.

One final point is worthy of your consideration. This last letter is not filled with "upbeat" comments on the glitz and glamour of the world and all that it promises you. Some people would insist that we "lighten up" and end these letters on a more positive note. They will contend that faithful Catholics take their religion too seriously.

Being tagged as a "doom-and-gloom killjoy" can be very uncomfortable. But the choice is yours. You can choose to follow the truth as taught to us by Our Lord and His Church or you can accept the secular world's view on how your life should be lived. Hopefully, you will choose the former and reject the latter.

Lastly, if you decide to be a true Catholic, there will be no compromises in following the teachings of your Faith. You will recall that Christ clearly made this point in the Gospel of Saint Matthew (12:30) when He stated, "He that is not with me is against me." Christ abhorred neutrality, particularly those "lukewarm" Catholics whom He equated as being vomit that He spewed from His mouth. This is a powerful image of how Our Lord feels about those who try "to sit on the fence" or "play both ends against the middle." Above all, don't let this characterization apply to you. As a Confirmed Catholic, you are a "Soldier for Christ." Remember, you are a disciple of Our Lord—"the salt of the earth" and "the light of the world." Stand your ground and be proud of the heritage that has been passed on to you.

To you, "the salt of the earth" and "the light of the world," I dedicate these Open Letters. Hopefully they will be of help in overcoming the many challenges ahead.

About the author

Paul Lavin received his Ph.D. in 1971. He is a clinical psychologist and the author of *Parenting the Overactive Child*.

Dr. Lavin also wrote three books on the Catholic Faith. *The Iron Man of China* is about his uncle, Father Joseph Lavin, who served as a Maryknoll priest for twenty years before his expulsion from China by the Communists. *Keeping the Faith: A Young Catholic's Guide to Coping with a Secular World* is for Catholic youth who will soon enter secular society. *Diabolical Satire: Satan's Response to the Conciliar Church* is a witty, satirical look at the revolutionary changes in the Catholic Church since Vatican II.

Lavin lives in Massachusetts and exclusively attends the traditional Latin Mass.

Rafka Press
Uplifting Families —
One Book at a Time

Visit our website for more Catholic literature
www.rafkapress.com

www.ingramcontent.com/pod-product-compliance
Lightning Source LLC
Chambersburg PA
CBHW022115040426
42450CB00006B/709